Planting *for* Wildlife

Planting *for* Wildlife

A Practical Guide to Restoring Native Woodlands

Nicola Munro and David Lindenmayer
Fenner School of Environment and Society, The Australian National University

PUBLISHING

Reprinted 2011, 2012

National Library of Australia Cataloguing-in-Publication entry

Munro, Nicola.

Planting for wildlife : a practical guide to restoring native woodlands/by Nicola Munro and David Lindenmayer.

9780643103122 (pbk.)
9780643103139 (epdf)
9780643103146 (epub)

Includes bibliographical references and index.

Woodlots – Australia.
Forest restoration – Australia.
Forests and forestry – Australia.
Revegetation – Australia.

Lindenmayer, David.

634.9560994

Published by
CSIRO PUBLISHING
36 Gardiner Road, Clayton VIC 3168
Private Bag 10, Clayton South VIC 3169
Australia

Telephone: [+613] 9545 8555
Local call: 1300 788 000 (Australia only)
Fax: +61 3 9662 7555
Email: csiropublishing@csiro.au
Web site: www.publishing.csiro.au

Front cover photos by (clockwise from main image): Nicola Munro, Nicola Munro, Dave Watts, Nicola Munro, Julian Robinson
Back cover photos by (clockwise from top right): Nicola Munro, Julian Robinson, Greening Australia

Set in Adobe Minion Pro 11/13.5 and Adobe Helvetica Neue LT
Edited by Anna Cutler
Cover and text design by James Kelly
Typeset by Desktop Concepts Pty Ltd, Melbourne
Index by Indexicana
Printed by Ingram Lightning Source

Feb26_RP_ILS

Contents

Preface

Across Australia, woodlands and forests are increasingly being planted on formerly cleared or semi-cleared land. Such revegetation efforts can be extremely positive for improving farm wildlife, enhancing aesthetics of the landscape, and even boosting farm production.

There has been some significant scientific and management research on revegetation in Australia over the past two decades. This guide book encompasses the latest information on restoring woodlands, with particular emphasis on plantings as habitat for wildlife. Key topics covered include why it is important to revegetate, where to plant, how to prepare a site, how to maintain and manage plantings, and how plantings change over time.

Much work remains to be done to increase the amount of land that is revegetated in Australia and improve the quality of restoration activities in areas that were once extensive woodland. Our sincere hope is that the information presented in this book will help achieve these important goals.

Nicola Munro and David Lindenmayer
April 2011

Acknowledgements

Claire Shepherd and Clive Hilliker assisted with a range of key tasks that made the initial concept of this book a reality. Dave Watts, Julian Robinson and a number of other colleagues kindly provided images for this book.

Our research on restored woodlands has been supported by many organisations over the past few decades. These include:

- The Murray Catchment Management Authority
- The Commonwealth Environmental Research Facility (CERF) (AEDA hub)
- The Australian Research Council
- Land and Water Australia
- The Natural Heritage Trust
- The Caring for our Country grants scheme (in collaboration with the Victorian Department of Sustainability and Environment)
- The North East Catchment Management Authority
- The Thomas Foundation
- The ACT Government
- The NSW Department of Environment, Climate Change and Water
- The Canberra Ornithologists Group
- The Bass Coast Landcare Network
- The Ecological Society of Australia.

David Lindenmayer would like to thank key members of his field team, particularly Mason Crane, Christopher MacGregor, Damian Michael, Rebecca Montague-Drake and Sachiko Okada. Nicola Munro thanks, in particular, Joern Fischer, Kimberlie Rawlings, Moragh McKay, Geoff Trease, Paul Spiers and Dave Blair for their role in improving revegetation for wildlife and learning how to be effective restorationists.

We thank John Manger from CSIRO Publishing, whose support and encouragement with this project is deeply appreciated.

1

Why revegetate?

Summary box

- This book focuses on revegetation of previously cleared woodland in south-eastern Australia. We focus on the south-eastern grazing region where domestic livestock grazing and/or cropping have been prominent forms of land use.
- These agricultural landscapes have suffered widespread land degradation and significant losses of biodiversity. Revegetation is a key step towards solving these problems.
- It is important to identify the main reasons for creating a planting before embarking on its design and establishment. This is because the underlying objectives will significantly influence its location, size, shape, composition and other aspects.

In this introductory chapter we discuss the key reasons why revegetation is important in Australian agricultural landscapes.

Australia's land use history

About 230 years ago, south-eastern Australia was covered in forests and woodlands that supported many species of animals and plants found nowhere else on Earth. Since European settlement, there have been enormous changes in this vast region. The development of agricultural land and exploitation of resources such as timber has resulted in extensive clearing of the original woodlands and forests (Fig. 1.1).

Figure 1.1. Cleared land that was formerly woodland in southern Victoria. (Photo by Nicola Munro)

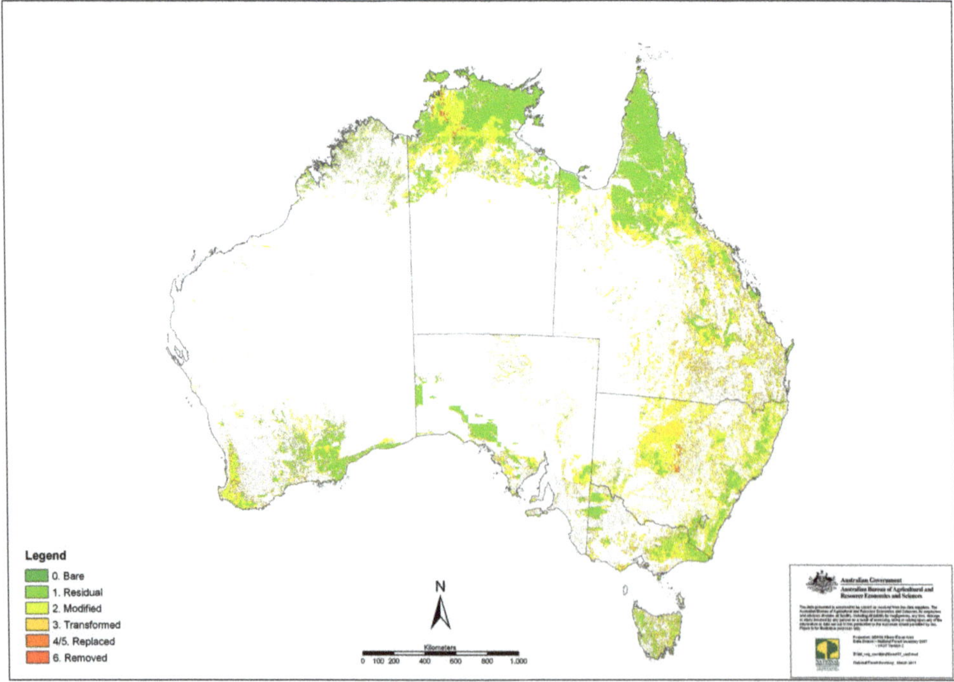

Figure 1.2. The extent of woodlands in Australia, indicating those that have been modified or recently cleared (replaced). The south-eastern grazing region was once predominantly woodland, much of which has been modified by agriculture. (Map prepared by Robert Dillon, DAFF)

Box 1.1. Australia's biodiversity decline

Australia has the unfortunate record of having the highest rate of recent mammal extinctions in the world (Fig. 1.3). Birds, reptiles, frogs and many other groups of organisms are also in decline. There are many reasons for the decline in Australia's wildlife, including loss of habitat, introduced predators (e.g. cats and foxes), introduced competitors (e.g. rabbits and goats) and other exotic species (e.g. Cane Toads), new diseases (e.g. Tasmanian Devil facial tumour), hunting, and altered fire regimes.

Throughout the agricultural regions of Australia, the loss of habitat is the single biggest problem facing our wildlife. 'Habitat' is the area, including all its resources, in which an animal lives. Many species are restricted to the 10–15% of native vegetation that has not been cleared in Australia's agricultural zone. However, much of this remaining vegetation is on low-productivity land, such as hilltops (Box 1.5), and is fragmented and degraded. Some animals will not cross large areas of open space (e.g. the Squirrel Glider), some are confined to large patches of native vegetation (e.g. the Eastern Yellow Robin), and others are strongly associated with vegetation in good condition (e.g. the Golden Whistler). Others require special features, such as old trees with hollows (e.g. parrots, possums and gliders), large logs (e.g. the Brown Treecreeper), leaf litter and surface rock (e.g. many reptiles), or dense understorey vegetation (e.g. ground-dwelling mammals, such as the native Bush Rat). Without these features, the animals that rely on them will not be present.

Vegetation clearing increases the isolation of remnant vegetation and reduces the size of patches, grazing reduces the quality of the vegetation and opens up the understorey, and cutting down old trees for firewood or clearing logs removes these important habitat features. Unfortunately, many common farming practices can lead to a loss of wildlife habitat. But there are also management actions, such as revegetation, that can re-create suitable habitat for many species.

Figure 1.3. The Tasmanian Bettong. This species was once widespread in the agricultural zones of eastern mainland Australia. It was an important 'ecosystem engineer' and its extensive diggings provided a range of key ecosystem functions, such as enabling rainfall to better penetrate the soil layer, promoting the germination of plants, and contributing to nutrient cycling. It is now found only in Tasmania. (Photo by Dave Watts)

Box 1.2. The Lanark property – a revegetation success story

Lanark is a sheep grazing property in the Western District of Victoria that has been totally transformed by a truly extraordinary revegetation program many decades ahead of its time. Like most properties in the district, it was extensively cleared of native vegetation in the mid to late 1800s. In response to widespread environmental degradation, the property owners, Cicely and John Fenton, with landscape architect Rochelle Rudduck, began a restoration program in 1967. Despite a dearth of information at the time, they established restoration plantings, shelterbelts and farm forestry plantations on approximately 11% of their property.

A local naturalist, Murray Gunn, began keeping records of the birds on Lanark in 1954. The bird records counted and compiled by Mr Gunn, Elizabeth Jacka and others spanned 40 years to 1996 and have become a valuable record of the changes in the bird assemblage.

There were an estimated 200 species of birds on Lanark prior to European settlement. In 1956 the property supported less than 40 species, mainly robust generalist species, such as the Red Wattlebird, Yellow-rumped Thornbill, Willie Wagtail, Australian Magpie and the Australian Raven. In the 20 years between 1956 and 1976, tree cover was increased from one to two per cent of the property. An estimated 46 species of birds recolonised the property including understorey-dependent birds such as the Brown Thornbill, Yellow-faced Honeyeater, Superb Fairy-wren, Eastern Spinebill, Golden Whistler and Grey Fantail. In addition, the establishment of wetlands facilitated the return of numerous water bird species. By 1996, 11% of the property was revegetated (Fig. 1.4), and a further 15 woodland bird species had colonised, including the Eastern Yellow Robin, White-browed Scrubwren, Pink Robin, Rufous Whistler, Rufous Fantail, Varied Sitella and the Bassian Thrush. In all, there were 75 bird species recorded in 1996.

About 85–90% of temperate woodland and forest has been replaced largely by cleared agricultural land (Fig. 1.2). Most remaining patches of remnant woodland and forest are small and fragmented. These patches are becoming increasingly degraded due to overgrazing by stock and feral animals, weed invasion, rising water tables, and excessive nutrients from fertiliser and livestock. These problems are causing tree dieback, reduced plant regeneration, and the decline or loss of populations of many species of native animals. They are also directly harming agricultural industries.

Against the backdrop of declining biodiversity and altered ecosystem condition is a large and growing number of people and organisations leading a revegetation revolution. Organisations such as Landcare, Greening Australia, and Catchment Management bodies are part of a very active movement to restore vegetation. Many thousands of dedicated people and millions of dollars have been spent on dozens of different schemes to collect native seed, establish native plant nurseries, and revegetate farms and other land. These efforts can have truly marked effects on the

Figure 1.4. An aerial photograph of revegetation at Lanark. (Photo by John and Cicely Fenton)

biodiversity and environmental condition of a property – as highlighted in the case of the Lanark farm in Box 1.2.

Why revegetate?

There are many reasons why land managers may want to revegetate land (see Table 1.1). The different reasons for revegetating can influence where a planting is situated, how big it is, and the composition of the restored vegetation. The first step in establishing a planting is to decide on its primary objectives and then rank these in order of importance. Is it a shelterbelt, for salinity control, to reduce stream bank erosion, to provide habitat for wildlife, or to sequester carbon? Many plantings will have multiple objectives, some of which may be mutually achievable, but others may require trade-offs.

Revegetation can help alleviate several land degradation problems and can have many benefits, as outlined in Table 1.1.

The scope of this book

The focus of our book is revegetation of woodlands in the agricultural landscapes of temperate south-eastern Australia. This is the area with which we are most

Box 1.3. Explanation of terms

There are a number of terms that describe revegetation, which we outline below.

Revegetation	Active restoration of native vegetation in a previously cleared area. This term is usually restricted to ecosystem restoration plantings, in which the revegetation resembles the original vegetation that was previously cleared. This can include planting seedlings or direct seeding, but does not include natural regeneration, gardens or the establishment of commercial plantations. This term is used almost only in Australia.
Reforestation	Active restoration of forests on previously cleared land. This term can also include the establishment of commercial plantations, or the regeneration of logging coupes.
Afforestation	This term is used mostly outside Australia, and is very similar to reforestation, but it does not assume that there was forest or woodland previously in the area to be planted (e.g. the area may have naturally been a grassland).
Restoration	Assisting the recovery of an ecosystem (that has been degraded or destroyed) toward its pre-degraded state. Revegetation is a form of restoration. Restoration can also include actions to promote the recovery of remnants, such as weeding, feral animal control, or soil improvement by reducing fertiliser use.
A planting	A new patch of trees, shrubs and sometimes other plants (Fig. 1.5). We use this term throughout the book for an area of revegetation.
Plantation	A tree crop that is managed (e.g. thinned, pruned) and then harvested for commercial purposes – in eucalypts, usually after 10 to 30 years.
Natural regeneration	The process of allowing or encouraging plants to regenerate without active planting (Fig. 1.5).
Rehabilitation and reclamation	Terms usually used for the restoration of mined land.

familiar because we have worked in it for almost 20 years. However, parts of this book also may be relevant to restorationists and land managers in south-western Australia. Although this book is focussed on woodlands, some of it will be relevant to forests. We do not discuss restoration of grasslands, wetlands, riparian areas, heath or rainforests, because restoration efforts in these ecosystems can differ from woodland revegetation. We also do not cover large-scale production forests, commercial plantations, farm forestry, or planted crops such as orchards. Finally, we have focussed much of this book on the benefits of revegetation for biodiversity because this is our area of expertise.

The chapters in this book encompass some of the key topics in revegetation, including: why revegetation is important (this chapter), where to locate a planting (Chapter 2), how to establish a planting (Chapter 3), what to plant (Chapter 4), ways to maintain and manage a planting (Chapter 5), and how plantings change over time (Chapter 6). These topics are clearly inter-related and there is unavoidable overlap in the content of some chapters.

Table 1.1. The benefits of revegetation

Prevent erosion	Plants can hold soil together, especially in steep or erosion-prone areas. Trees and shrubs hold soil together at a greater depth than grasses. Plant cover reduces the impact of raindrops and slows the flow of water during heavy rain.
Stabilise stream banks	Plants provide structural stability along the edges of rivers and streams.
Improve water quality	Plants along streams and rivers reduce the amount of topsoil entering the water. Waterborne soil particles can cause erosion downstream because 'dirty water' is abrasive. Plant cover along streams can also reduce the amount of fertiliser, other chemicals and nutrients entering the water.
Windbreaks	Trees and shrubs create windbreaks that can reduce evaporation from the soil on the lee side, and limit wind erosion. Crop yields are often higher on the lee side of windbreaks.
Shade for stock	Stock congregate under shade trees during hot weather. Stock that are not heat stressed gain weight faster and drink less water than those with limited access to shade (Fig. 1.6).
Reduce salinity problems	Plants, especially trees, absorb groundwater and if planted strategically in the landscape can reduce recharge. Salt-tolerant species can be planted on salt-affected land to lower water tables and help control salinity.
Provide habitat for wildlife	Plantings provide habitat for wildlife and connectivity between remnant patches.
Provide timber and firewood	Planted trees can eventually be harvested for timber and firewood.
Reduce insect loads in pastures	Many of the bird species that inhabit plantings eat insects in pastures, such as blowflies and the larvae of scarab beetles. Reduced populations of these insects can improve pasture and stock health.
Provide forage for stock	Plantings can be designed for future browsing by stock and provide an alternative food source during times of low pasture productivity.
Improve tree health	Plantings surrounding old remnant trees attract birds, which eat insects that damage trees, reducing tree dieback.
Tackle climate change	Trees and shrubs are important long-term stores of carbon, which will help lower the current elevated carbon levels in the atmosphere. Trees do this better than grasses because they are bigger and live longer, and therefore store more carbon for longer.
Provide non-timber forest products	Non-timber forest products in a planting can include cut flowers, medicinal herbs, fragrant oils, or craft products (e.g. seed pods, leaves, branches, feathers, flowers, and reeds).
Increase local rainfall	There is some evidence that woodlands and forests change local climatic conditions and can increase local rainfall.
Stewardship payments	There is a global trend toward paying landholders to conserve remnant native vegetation on their land and/or to establish revegetated areas on their land. Several schemes in Australia now provide landholders with conservation-related stewardship payments. An example is the Box Gum Grassy Woodland Stewardship Program administered by the Australian Government.
Provide natural history interest	Many people are interested in natural history. Revegetation can facilitate an interest in local natural history, particularly because it provides habitat for many species of animals.
Create aesthetically pleasing landscapes	To many, landscapes with trees and shrubs look better than treeless paddocks.
Positive for human wellbeing	The act of restoring native environments is a positive experience for most people. There is considerable evidence of the benefit of nature and restorative actions on the human psyche.

Figure 1.5. A planting and natural regeneration. (Photos by Nicola Munro)

Figure 1.6. Plantings can provide excellent shelter for stock. (Photo by David Lindenmayer)

Figure 1.7. A wide range of species play key ecosystem roles in Australian woodlands. For example, bats, birds, small mammals and invertebrates contribute significantly to pollination and seed dispersal. (Photos by Julian Robinson and Nicola Munro)

Box 1.4. Ecosystem services

Ecosystem services are the resources and processes provided by natural ecosystems. They are the services that we depend on for our survival and quality of life (Fig. 1.7). They can be divided into four groups:

- *Provisioning services,* such as the production of food, timber and water.
- *Regulating services,* such as the control of climate, disease, water quality and air quality.
- *Supporting services,* such as nutrient cycles and crop pollination.
- *Cultural services,* such as spiritual and recreational benefits.

The economics of ecosystem services is complex. Some people advocate putting a dollar value on all ecosystem services; however, agreeing on a price is difficult. For example, does a single tree cost a few dollars from a nursery, or should the cost include the clean air provided by the tree, the tree's contribution to reducing salinity, its contribution to carbon storage, and the biodiversity that resides on the tree? A remnant patch can be priced on its provisioning services (e.g. the value of timber), or on the cost of restoration or management (e.g. weeding or supplementary planting), or the cost of creation (e.g. the cost of the seedlings, fences and tree guards). Despite these difficulties surrounding price, a monetary value of some sort is required for stewardship payments. These are payments to a landholder for establishing plantings on their land but which benefit all of society because of the ecosystem services they provide. Stewardship payments are common in Europe and have recently begun to be established in Australia.

Box 1.5. Not all parts of landscapes are created equal – the non-uniform pattern of vegetation clearing

Australia's woodland ecosystems have not all been cleared to the same degree. Types of woodland that typically occur on rocky hilltops have often been left, while woodland on flat land and valley floors, which often have productive soils, have been extensively cleared (Fig. 1.8). On productive land, the only remnants left are often along roadsides, streams, in cemeteries, travelling stock reserves, or as scattered remnant trees in paddocks. One problem with this situation is that the more productive valley floors were also more productive for biodiversity before settlement by non-indigenous people. Therefore, most of the vegetation remaining after extensive clearing is in low-productivity areas, where trees grow slowly and populations of many animal species are small.

Figure 1.8. Hilltops were often left uncleared because they are less productive than flatter land. Flatter, productive parts of the landscape were often heavily cleared and now have very little remnant vegetation. (Photo by Nicola Munro)

Why this book was written

Over the past two decades, many landholders have asked us about the best way to establish plantings on their farm and whether their plantings do provide habitat for wildlife. While there are a number of excellent books on restoration of other ecosystems, such as wetlands and rainforests, there is currently no practical guide book on revegetation of woodlands. We felt it was important for there to be a short, pithy and practical guide available that focuses closely on the key aspects of revegetation.

References

Fenton J (2010) *The Untrained Environmentalist.* Allen & Unwin, Sydney.

O'Neill G (1999) Renaissance on Lanark. *Wingspan Supplement* **9**: 1–16.

Vesk PA and Mac Nally R (2006) The clock is ticking – revegetation and habitat for birds and arboreal mammals in rural landscapes of southern Australia. *Agriculture, Ecosystems and Environment* **112**: 356–366.

White M (1994) *After the Greening: The Browning of Australia.* Kangaroo Press, Kenthurst, NSW.

White M (1997) *Listen ... Our Land Is Crying: Australia's Environment: Problems and Solutions.* Kangaroo Press, Kenthurst, NSW.

2

Where to revegetate

Summary box

- There are three key scales that influence where to establish a planting – the regional scale, the landscape scale and the farm scale.
- At the regional scale, it is important to prioritise the location of plantings to control salinity and groundwater recharge.
- At the landscape scale, it is important to consider connectivity for wildlife and representation of different kinds of ecosystems.
- At the farm scale, it is important to consider opportunities to enlarge or enhance existing areas of plantings and areas of native vegetation.

After the main objectives of a planting have been identified and prioritised (see Chapter 1), the next step is to determine where to locate a planting. This chapter outlines the different factors that need to be considered when planning where to plant at the regional, landscape and farm scales. We define these scales as follows:

- Regional scale – equivalent to Catchment Management Authority (CMA) regions.
- Landscape scale – approximately 10 by 10 kilometres (100 km^2).
- Farm scale – up to about 2000 hectares (20 km^2).

Often, different people will make decisions at each scale. For example, a state authority may make decisions about where to allocate funding for plantings at a regional scale. Within each region, a local natural resource manager may make decisions about where to establish revegetation at a landscape scale. Farmers or landholders will make decisions about where to plant on a farm. Revegetation programs are important at all scales because work at one will reinforce the effectiveness of planting efforts at another.

Where to plant at a regional scale

At a regional scale, plantings should be located where they will be most effective in reducing water tables to control dryland salinity, and integrating with remnant vegetation.

Where to plant to control salinity

Salinity is a complex issue. In salt-affected areas, more water needs to be used by vegetation at the regional scale to ameliorate the salinity problem. Trees do this much better than annual crops or pasture (Fig. 2.1). Therefore, one of the main regional-scale objectives of plantings in salt-affected areas is to reduce the amount of rainfall moving past plant roots and reaching the groundwater.

When rainfall leaks into the groundwater it is called 'recharge', and the area in the catchment in which this occurs is called the 'recharge area'. The 'discharge area' of a catchment is where the groundwater comes to the surface (e.g. as seeps).

One of the best ways to tackle the problem of dryland salinity is to plant trees on previously cleared land. Planting in the recharge area is thought to be the best way to reduce recharge to the water table, and planting in the discharge area to

Box 2.1. Dryland salinity

Clearing vegetation can lead to dryland salinity. Patterns of hydrology under agricultural systems are very different from those under the original native vegetation. Prior to clearing, native vegetation used most of the rainfall and there was limited seepage into the groundwater. The salt was stored deep in the soil layer. After conversion to shallow-rooted crops and grasses, much more rainfall penetrated below the root zone, leaking into the groundwater and causing the water table to rise, mobilising salt. When a water table rises close to the root zone, the vegetation becomes waterlogged and salt-affected (Fig. 2.2). Sometimes the water table can reach the surface and cause salt scalds.

Although we know what causes dryland salinity, it is still a struggle to determine the best way to fix the problem. Putting more trees back in the landscape is certainly part of the solution, but studies have estimated that 16–22% of a catchment may need to be revegetated to reduce rates of groundwater recharge. In some places, entire landscapes may need revegetating. Deep-rooted crops, such as lucerne or tree plantations, are showing promise in helping to reduce water tables. However, growing trees requires a lot of water and, ironically, there may not be sufficient rainfall to support many planted trees.

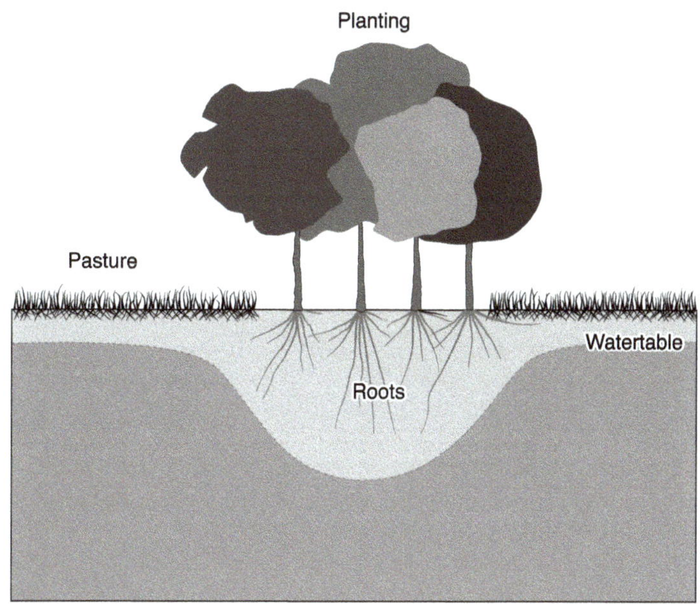

Figure 2.1. The water table is lower under trees than under annual crops or pasture. (Figure by Clive Hilliker, adapted from Stirzaker *et al.* 2002)

reduce elevated water tables. However, some areas may respond quickly to revegetation, whereas others may respond more slowly. This is because groundwater behaves differently depending on factors such as soil type, geological

Figure 2.2. A rising water table carries salt to the surface, which then causes salt scald and tree death. (Photo by David Lindenmayer)

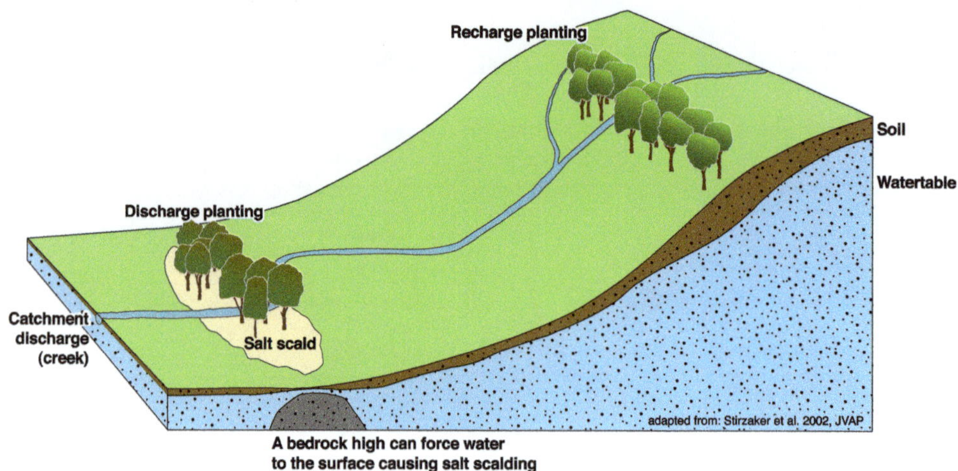

Figure 2.3. Cross section of a slope showing plantings located to control groundwater recharge and discharge. (Figure by Clive Hilliker, adapted from Stirzaker *et al.* 2002)

formation, topography, the depth of the water table, the amount of salt in the soil, and the amount of discharge in the form of streams and rivers. It is important to know about the local groundwater, and local government authorities or CMAs should have this information.

In small local catchments, typically at the edge of ranges and higher hills, tree belts or widely scattered trees can often control groundwater recharge with a relatively small area of land converted to plantings (Fig. 2.3). In many cases this is the most effective control of dryland salinity, but the number of areas in Australia in which it can be done is small. In large catchments (e.g. valleys or flat plains), extensive areas may need to be revegetated to achieve a significant reduction in groundwater recharge. Plantings in a discharge area can help to lower water tables, but in some cases salt accumulates in the root zone of plants, eventually causing them to die. Discharge areas need to be planted with salt-tolerant plants, but even these have limits to the amount of salt they can tolerate. Planting in the discharge area is most effective where the groundwater is shallow, the water is not too saline, and where there is sideways movement of water to prevent salt accumulation at the roots. Large, badly salt-affected catchments may need other remediation works to control groundwater and salinity, such as deep drains or groundwater pumping.

Where to plant to integrate with remnant vegetation

Revegetation can enhance, enlarge or connect remnant patches of native vegetation (Figs. 2.4 and 2.5). Patches of remnant native vegetation are critical for the conservation of wildlife. Regional-scale connectivity can be increased by establishing revegetation patches that act as stepping stones for wildlife, or by

Figure 2.4. This planting both enlarges and connects with the remnant vegetation on the hilltop. (Photo by David Lindenmayer)

enhancing natural corridors of vegetation, such as along rivers or roads. Wildlife is predicted to benefit from enhanced regional-scale connectivity (see Box 2.2); however, little research has been done on this topic.

Regional-scale connectivity is likely to be particularly important in this era of rapid climate change because some native plants and animals may need to disperse large distances to find new climatically suitable areas. Several regional-scale

Figure 2.5. This young planting in Gippsland connects with the remnant in the background, enlarging the entire patch of vegetation. (Photo by Dave Blair)

Box 2.2. The Gondwana Link project

The Gondwana Link project is an ambitious program tackling connectivity at a regional scale. The project is located in south-west Western Australia and aims to reconnect vegetation from the wet forests in the far south-west of the state to the edge of the Nullarbor Plain (Fig. 2.6). This 1000-km arc currently consists of a string of disconnected areas of remnant vegetation (mostly national parks). The aim of the Gondwana Link project is to connect the existing patches by filling the gaps with revegetation. These gaps are being filled by revegetation on a grand scale on agricultural properties that have been bought by conservation agencies and on private land.

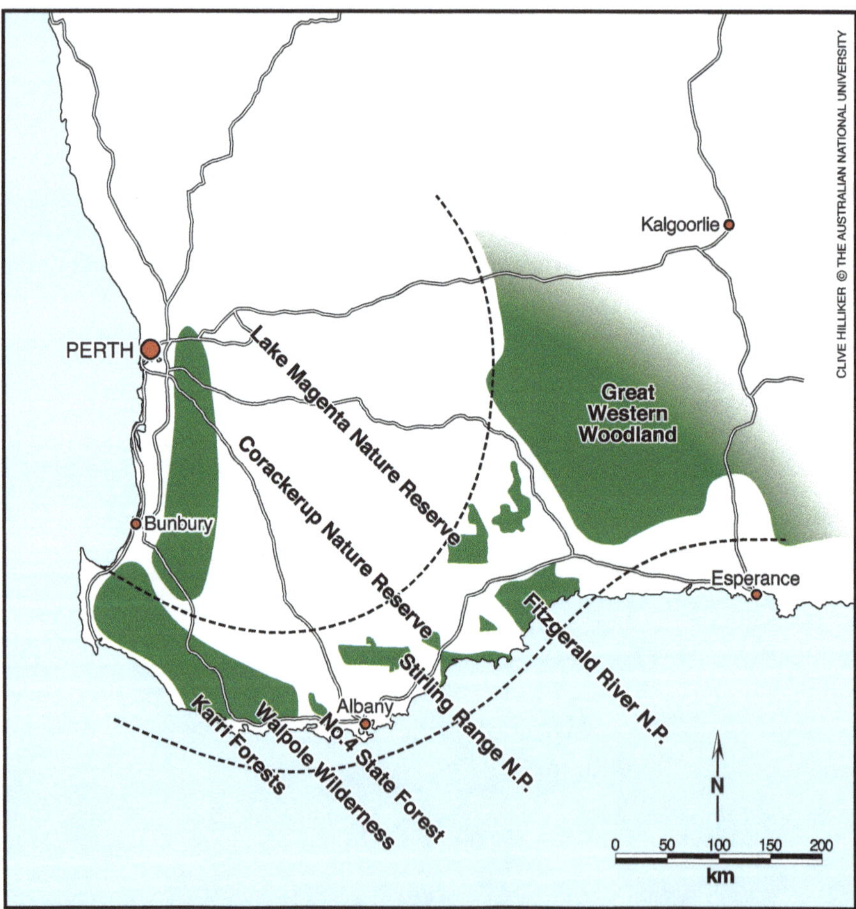

Figure 2.6. A map of the Gondwana Link project showing major existing remnant vegetation in south-west Western Australia. The dotted lines are the 'boundaries' of the Gondwana Link project. (Figure by Clive Hilliker)

Box 2.3. Habitat 141

Habitat 141 is an inspirational project with a vision to reconnect vegetation at a regional scale. Habitat 141 is located along the Victorian–South Australian border, and aims to establish a large corridor of vegetation between the Murray River and the southern coastline. This will span about 700 km and link several large national parks that include the Grampians, Little Desert, Wyperfeld and Murray-Sunset. Most of the revegetation work in this project is being conducted on private farmland, although one property has been purchased for revegetation. Many farmers and communities have embraced the challenge of connecting the 'ocean to the outback'. To date, one million trees and plants have been planted or direct seeded.

restoration programs have recently been initiated, including the Gondwana Link project (Box 2.2) and Habitat 141 (Box 2.3).

Where to plant at the landscape scale

Two key considerations should influence the design and location of plantings at the landscape scale: connectivity and representation of different kinds of ecosystems. Plantings that increase connectivity across a landscape should be a high priority. Connectivity can be enhanced by long linear plantings (such as along creek or river banks; Fig. 2.8), or by creating 'stepping stones' through a landscape. 'Stepping stones' are patches of vegetation that are close enough together to enable most animals to move from one patch to the next.

At a landscape scale, decisions can be made on where to place a planting based on the representation of different ecosystems. Box 1.4 in Chapter 1 describes how most clearing has taken place in productive flat areas and on valley floors. Conversely, most of the larger remnant vegetation patches (e.g. many reserves) are located on low-productivity hilltops. Often hilltops and valley floors support distinct ecosystems with different suites of animals and plants. Therefore, it is particularly important to revegetate the more heavily cleared vegetation types found in flat areas (Fig. 2.10).

Where to plant at the farm scale

The farm is the scale at which most landholders make decisions about where to establish a planting. Landholders should take into account such factors as existing areas of remnant native vegetation, existing plantings, fences, roads, creek lines and buildings (Fig. 2.11). Plantings that buffer, enlarge, enhance or connect remnant vegetation will be of greatest benefit for biodiversity.

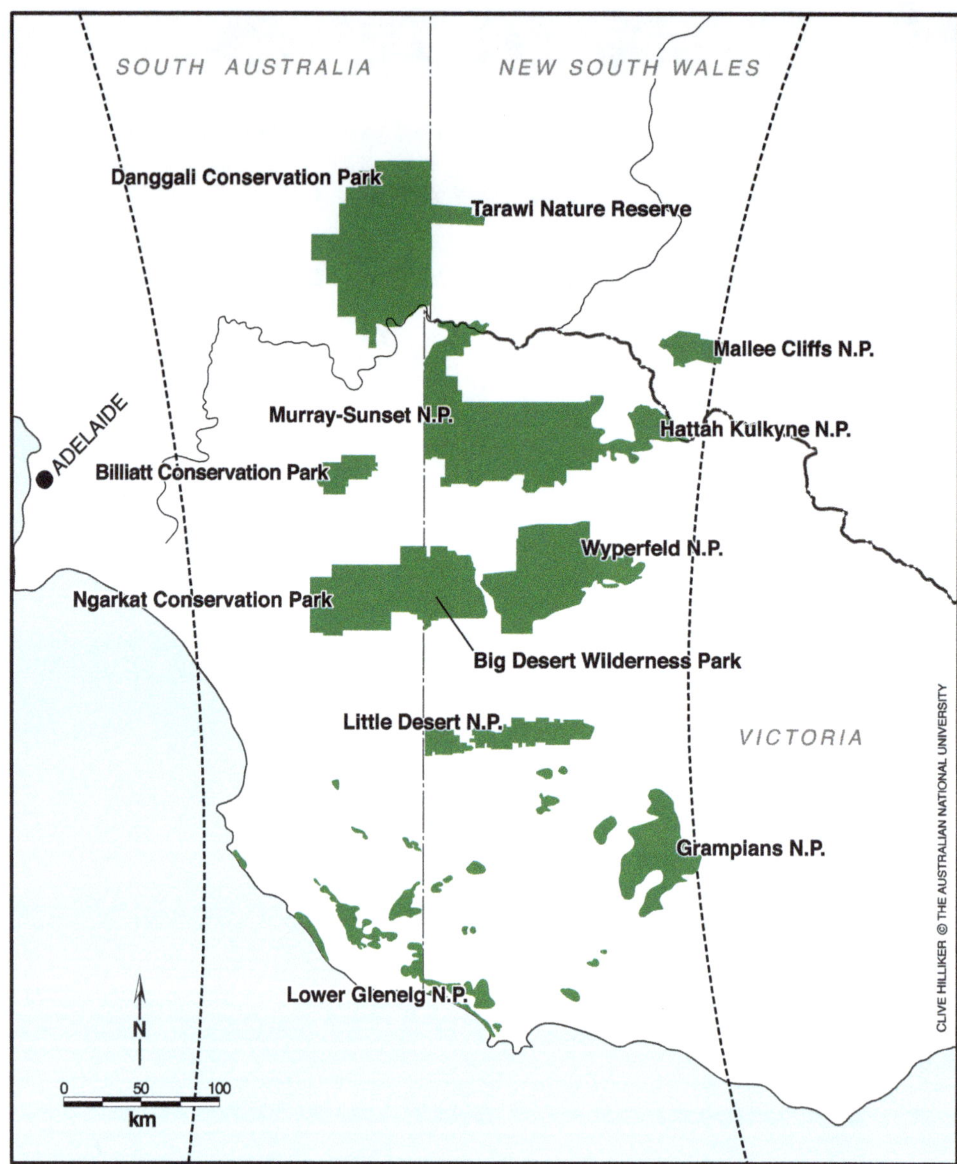

Figure 2.7. A map of the Habitat 141 project showing major existing remnant vegetation on the South Australia–Victoria border. The dotted lines are the 'boundaries' of the Habitat 141 project. (Figure by Clive Hilliker)

Existing patches of remnant native vegetation should be a key focus for protection in agricultural landscapes. Even very small patches of remnant vegetation (e.g. isolated paddock trees) are valuable. However, small patches are also vulnerable. They are prone to disturbances (such as fire or storms), contain small populations of plants and animals (which are prone to extinction), and may

Figure 2.8. This linear planting starts at the headwaters of a small creek and crosses several farms. Connected plantings can be established when neighbouring landholders work together. (Photo by Nicola Munro)

Figure 2.9. A Marbled Gecko and a Brown Treecreeper – species with markedly different perspectives of connectivity in the same landscape. (Photos by Nicola Munro and Julian Robinson)

Box 2.4. What is connectivity?

Ecologists often talk about increasing landscape connectivity, but what does this mean? Connectivity is, in theory, best defined from the perspective of the species of animal or plant being managed or studied (Fig. 2.9). However, in practice, landscapes are usually examined and managed from a human perspective. Establishing linear plantings that connect patches of vegetation may not lead to improved connectivity for a forest snail but it may do so for species that perceive the landscape at a similar scale to humans (e.g. some species of birds).

The objective of increasing connectivity in a landscape is to increase opportunities for animals and plants to move or disperse. Animals may move short distances around their home range, or over large distances when dispersing or migrating. Young animals often need to move away from the home range of their parents to reduce competition for resources. If movement is hindered, problems can occur, such as genetic inbreeding or localised extinction if, for example, a fire burns a patch and recolonisation cannot occur.

Many woodland and forest animals are reluctant to cross extensive areas of open agricultural land. Paddocks can be dangerous places because there is no cover to hide from predators (e.g. owls, foxes), and there may be no resources (e.g. food) along the way. While a few species have adapted to open spaces, many have a limited distance they will cross over open paddocks.

Field-based research has shown that some animals will move through corridors of vegetation in preference to open paddocks, and that isolated paddock trees are used as stepping stones by some species of birds. However, there has been only limited research to date on the long-term benefits to wildlife of a relatively connected landscape compared with a disconnected one. In addition, there may be potential problems associated with increasing connectivity, such as promoting the movement of introduced animals (e.g. the Red Fox). In general, however, it is usually considered beneficial to wildlife to ensure gaps between patches of vegetation do not exceed a few hundred metres.

not provide all the resources required by animals all of the time (e.g. flowering or seeding episodes or tree hollows for breeding). Therefore, plantings that enlarge existing remnants should be a high priority for establishment.

Plantings next to or around existing patches of remnant native vegetation have a buffering effect and reduce the amount of wind and spray-drift reaching a remnant.

Plantings can have different values for biodiversity depending on their juxtaposition with other plantings and patches of remnant native vegetation. Recent research has shown that plantings established near each other or close to existing remnant native woodland support more species of birds and are more likely to support a range of bird species (Fig. 2.12). This is because the combination

Figure 2.10. Plantings on the largely cleared, highly productive parts of the landscape are particularly important for biodiversity. (Photo by David Lindenmayer)

of remnant vegetation and planted native vegetation provides habitat for more species and/or facilitates movement between habitat patches.

Some patches of remnant vegetation on farms could benefit from enhancement plantings (see Box 4.1). Remnants that are grazed usually lack native understorey, so fencing remnants and planting native understorey species may benefit wildlife.

Plantings on farms can be used to connect patches of native vegetation or other revegetation plantings. Plantings along creeks and rivers or along roadsides form natural corridors. Many landholders place long linear plantings beside existing fences. Because only the other side of the planting then needs to be fenced, costs are reduced. Linear plantings can also function as windbreaks (see Box 3.1), which benefit stock and adjacent crops.

Plantings on a farm can include restoration of scattered tree landscapes (Fig. 2.13). This is not a widely used practice, but can benefit both wildlife and farm enterprises. Scattered paddock trees provide connectivity for wildlife. They also provide shade for stock. Disadvantages of planting scattered trees are that they may be difficult to establish (e.g. under set stock grazing conditions), can be costly to fence (if each one has to be fenced individually), and are usually composed of only tree species (no shrubs or ground cover plants). An innovative way to establish more trees scattered throughout paddocks has been devised by Greening Australia, called Whole of Paddock Rehabilitation (see Box 2.6).

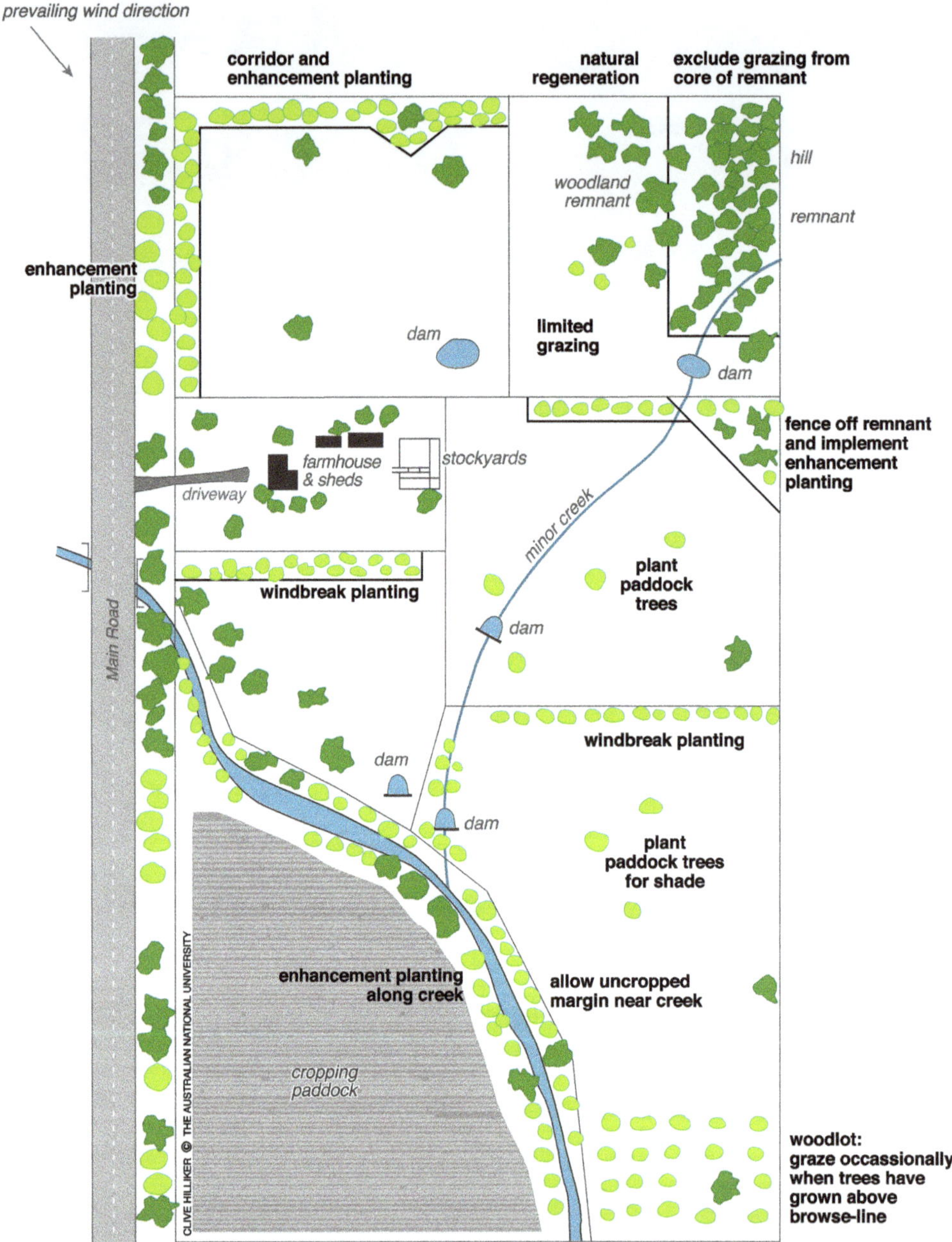

Figure 2.11. An example farm plan for revegetation. Dark green indicates existing remnant trees. Pale green indicates newly planted trees. (Figure by Clive Hilliker)

Revegetation at multiple spatial scales

In summary, regional planners need to prioritise plantings to make the greatest contribution to the control of salinity, and also enhance connectivity for wildlife.

Figure 2.12. The Rufous Whistler and Grey Fantail are examples of species that can benefit from plantings near remnants. (Photos by Julian Robinson)

Resource managers or planners at a landscape scale need to address issues of connectivity and the representation of different vegetation communities. Farmers need to plan their new plantings to complement existing plantings and areas of remnant native vegetation as well as promote farm-scale connectivity.

The amount of vegetation in a region, landscape or farm is by far the most important factor influencing the presence, abundance and species richness of biodiversity. Researchers have suggested that a minimum threshold of 30% native

Box 2.5. Where and when not to plant

Just as there are key areas where plantings are likely to be most effective, there are also certain parts of farms best avoided. For example, intact areas of native grassland are very important habitats, so it is inappropriate to establish plantings on them. However, many areas of open grazing country are native secondary grasslands (which occur where woodland has been cleared), in which plantings may be beneficial if established with relevant local native species. Similarly, rocky areas can be critically important environments for species-rich groups of native reptiles and planting programs in these areas need to be carefully considered. Dense plantings in rocky areas can be particularly detrimental because of changes to the amount of incoming solar radiation and, consequently, thermal conditions for reptiles.

Restoration of tree cover through an active program of tree planting might be best achieved on parts of farms where there has been high grazing pressure or a prolonged history of fertiliser application. However, it is important to carefully weigh up when it is appropriate to instigate a planting program and when re-establishing vegetation cover may be best achieved by letting natural regeneration occur. The most successful natural tree regeneration will occur in areas of a farm that are:

- within approximately two tree heights of living trees, and
- subject to limited grazing pressure from domestic livestock, and
- where there has been an absence or limited past history of fertiliser application.

Figure 2.13. Although not commonly done, it can be beneficial to plant paddock trees as they make excellent stepping stones through the landscape for wildlife. (Photo by David Lindenmayer)

Figure 2.14. Whole of Paddock Rehabilitation (WOPR) is a scheme by Greening Australia to establish scattered trees across a large area. (Photo by Greening Australia Capital Region)

Box 2.6. Whole of Paddock Rehabilitation (WOPR)

Whole of Paddock Rehabilitation is an innovative approach developed by Greening Australia to establish scattered trees and shrubs throughout paddocks (Fig. 2.14). It is an effective way to provide new habitat for wildlife and enhance connectivity on a relatively large scale. Whole of Paddock Rehabilitation also has beneficial outcomes for agricultural production (see below).

Under the WOPR program, graziers volunteer a paddock of at least 10 ha for revegetation. Greening Australia then establishes trees and shrubs by direct seeding in widely spaced strips in the paddock. A stewardship payment of $50 per hectare per year is offered to the grazier, with half paid upfront and half paid at the end of five years. After five years, the grazier can reintroduce stock to the paddock under a rotational grazing system. This scheme is particularly suited to paddocks already requiring rehabilitation.

The key benefits of this scheme include carbon sequestration, salinity and erosion control, and little or no fencing costs. Whole of Paddock Rehabilitation also enables the regeneration of native grasses and other plants. Wildlife benefits from the additional vegetation and enhanced landscape connectivity. There are also production benefits, such as provision of shade and shelter for stock, seed pods and foliage from wattles for fodder, and soil improvement through increased nitrogen fixation and nutrient cycling. Recent research has found that stock consumption of *Acacia* seed pods by sheep can increase resistance to internal parasites.

vegetation in a landscape may be required to sustain biodiversity. While biodiversity is likely to be enhanced by at least 30% native vegetation cover in all landscapes, there is limited scientific evidence that this is a critical amount above

Box 2.7. Paddock tree decline and lack of tree regeneration

Remnant trees on farms are often old – many are a legacy from before settlement by non-indigenous people. Many eucalypts have a maximum lifespan of 400 to 500 years. Across the temperate agricultural zone, these paddock trees are dying of old age and are not being replaced by natural regeneration. Few are forecast to remain in 30 to 40 years time. If farming practices change to encourage natural tree regeneration, the rate of tree and biodiversity loss could be dramatically slowed.

Recent research has shown that natural regeneration of paddock trees can occur if farmers adopt short rotation grazing with long rest periods (e.g. each paddock grazed for less than 90 days per year), and limit the use of fertiliser. Many farmers are now adopting this kind of grazing. Encouraging natural tree regeneration is a lot cheaper than planting trees in revegetation programs. But in the absence of natural tree regeneration, plantings may be the only viable restoration option.

which biodiversity is sustained. In general, the more vegetation in a landscape, the better that landscape is likely to be for biodiversity.

References

Dorrough J and Moxham C (2005) Eucalypt establishment in agricultural landscapes and implications for landscape-scale restoration. *Biological Conservation* **123**: 55–66.

Fischer J and Lindenmayer DB (2002) The conservation value of paddock trees for birds in a variegated landscape in southern New South Wales. 2. Paddock trees as stepping stones. *Biodiversity and Conservation* **11**: 833–849.

Fischer J, Stott J, Zerger A, Warren G, Sherren K and Forrester RI (2009) Reversing a tree regeneration crisis in an endangered ecoregion. *Proceedings of the National Academy of Sciences* **106**: 10386–10391.

Gibbons P, Lindenmayer DB, Fischer J, Manning AD, Weinberg A, Sedden J, Ryan P and Barrett G (2008) The future of scattered trees in agricultural landscapes. *Conservation Biology* **22**: 1309–1319.

Gibbons P and Boak M (2002) The value of paddock trees for regional conservation in an agricultural landscape. *Ecological Management and Restoration* **3**: 205–210.

Manning AD, Fischer J and Lindenmayer DB (2006) Scattered trees are keystone structures - implications for conservation. *Biological Conservation* **132**: 311-321.

Stirzaker R, Vertessy R and Sarre A (Eds) (2002) *Trees, Water and Salt: An Australian Guide to Using Trees for Healthy Catchments and Productive Farms.* Joint Venture Agroforestry Program. Rural Industries Research and Development Corporation, Canberra.

Stirzaker RJ, Cook FJ and Knight JH (1999) Where to plant trees on cropping land for control of dryland salinity: some approximate solutions. *Agricultural Water Management* **39**: 115–133.

Turner NC and Ward PR (2002) The role of agroforestry and perennial pasture in mitigating water logging and secondary salinity: summary. *Agricultural Water Management* **53**: 271–275.

3

Layout and composition of a planting

Summary box

- The larger and wider a planting, the better it will be for biodiversity.
- The more similar a planting is to the structure and composition of pre-cleared vegetation, the better it will be for biodiversity.
- The density of a planting should match the original remnant vegetation in the area.
- The biodiversity value of a planting will be increased if it includes old paddock trees, logs and rocks.

Once the location of a planting has been chosen (see Chapter 2), the next steps are to determine:

- the size and shape of a planting,
- which species to plant,
- the spacing of plants, and
- what other features to include.

These key steps in determining the layout of a planting are the primary topics of this chapter.

Size, width and shape of a planting

The dimensions of a planting may be dictated by a number of other farm decisions. A planting intended to primarily act as a windbreak may be long and narrow in

Box 3.1. The effectiveness of windbreaks

High wind speeds can cause erosion, high rates of evaporation, reduced crop production, and stress in livestock. Belts of trees can effectively reduce wind speeds, providing protection for a horizontal distance of about 12 times their height.

A windbreak needs to be located where it blocks prevailing winds. Where winds are not consistent in direction, planting windbreaks around the perimeter of a paddock may be an option. Windbreaks composed of only trees can form gaps under the canopy as the trees mature (Fig. 3.2), which create a wind tunnelling effect that negates protection. Shrubs planted in a windbreak can prevent wind tunnelling.

However, a completely impermeable windbreak can create eddies on the lee side, which reduces wind protection, so windbreaks should be semi-permeable for maximum effect (Fig. 3.1). Again, this is best achieved with a combination of trees and shrubs. Eucalypts, casuarinas and other Australian native trees make better semi-permeable windbreaks than dense conifers, such as cypress hedges.

shape, allowing minimal land to be taken out of production (see Box 3.1). Alternatively, an entire paddock may be set aside for a planting proposed for conservation or salinity control (see Box 2.6 on Whole of Paddock Rehabilitation). Below, we describe several of the benefits and limitations of different sizes, widths and shapes of plantings.

Size of a planting

Species richness is usually higher in large plantings than in small plantings (Fig. 3.3). In general, large plantings are likely to support more species of plants and animals than small plantings, as they tend to provide a greater range of habitats. For example, a large planting may contain a variety of topographical features (gullies, ridges, slopes, flat areas, creeks) that have subtly different microclimates, which affect vegetation composition, and subsequently, animal species composition. It is beneficial to establish plantings with a variety of environmental conditions, such as water-associated species along creeks or gullies or leaving small open areas within plantings. In addition, some plants and animals prefer to live in large patches of vegetation. However, a large planting is not guaranteed to have greater variation in conditions or species richness than a small planting. For example, a woodlot may be homogenous in structure and plant species composition and therefore may support few species of native plants and animals.

Large plantings are a cost effective way to revegetate areas of land. For example, it is cheaper (particularly for fencing costs), to revegetate 10 ha in a single block planting, than 10 ha of land as narrow strips or small patches throughout a farm.

The biggest cause of biodiversity decline in Australia is loss of habitat; a key solution is to increase the amount of habitat. If planting large patches results in the

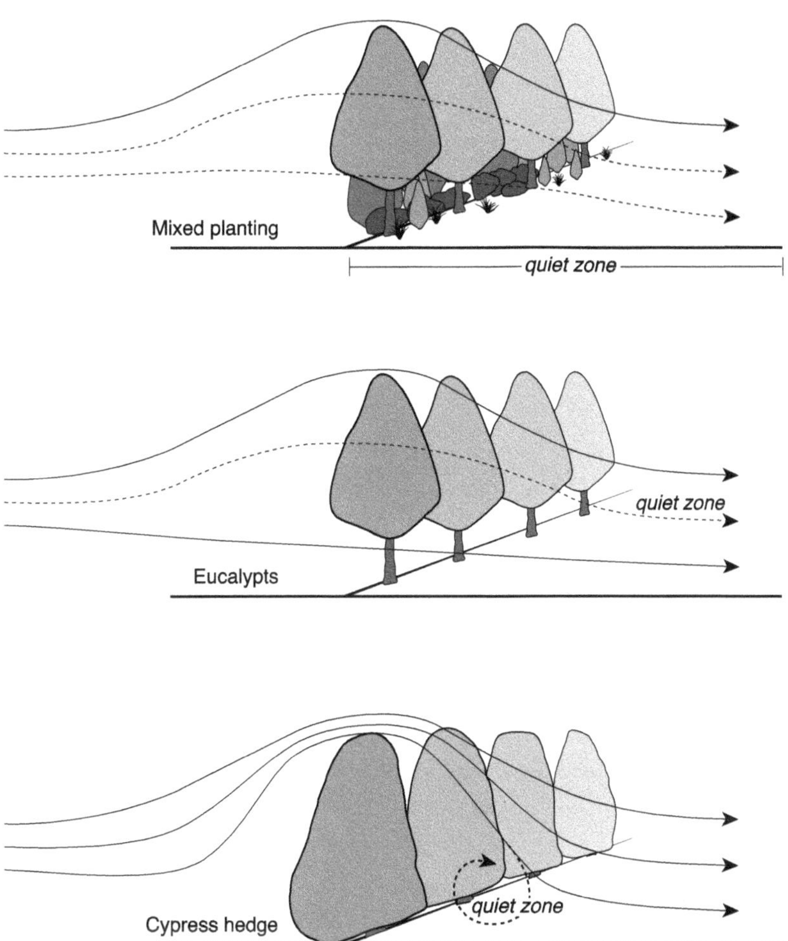

Figure 3.1. A semi-permeable windbreak (top) provides the best protection from wind erosion. Gaps under the canopy can cause wind tunnelling (middle). Dense vegetation can cause the wind to eddy on the lee side (bottom). (Figure by Clive Hilliker)

establishment of a greater total area of revegetation, then this is likely to be positive for biodiversity.

Width of a planting

All patches of vegetation have an edge area and an interior area or core. The edge area is a zone, commonly degraded, in which wind, light and spray-drift may enter a patch and alter plant and animal communities. It may be several metres (or even up to 50 m) deep, depending on the type of impact and type of vegetation. The edge and the interior provide different habitat that suits different species. For example, some species of weed, such as Sweet Pittosporum outside its natural range, thrive at the edges of patches but do not occur in the interior. Conversely, some animals prefer to live in the core of a patch and/or breed more successfully there.

Figure 3.2. A young, narrow planting of only trees showing a gap under the canopy. (Photo by Nicola Munro)

Figure 3.3. A large block planting. (Photo by Nicola Munro)

Wide plantings have greater benefits for biodiversity than narrow plantings, for similar reasons as described above for the size of a planting. A narrow planting can be dominated by edge conditions (Fig. 3.4). Animals likely to live in a narrow planting include edge specialists, such as the Yellow-rumped Thornbill (Fig. 3.5), and generalists, such as the Australian Magpie. However, more species of birds inhabit wide (>20 m) than narrow (<10 m) plantings. The effects of the width of a planting on other groups of animals are less well known.

Narrow, linear plantings are common in agricultural landscapes because they are often easier to accommodate in farm planning than large block plantings. Linear plantings can be effective windbreaks (see Box 3.1), and can provide movement corridors for wildlife. Linear plantings along creeks and rivers can be important habitats for animals, help stabilise stream banks, prevent erosion, and

Figure 3.4. A narrow strip planting. (Photo by Nicola Munro)

Figure 3.5. A Yellow-rumped Thornbill, an edge-specialist species in plantings. (Photo by Julian Robinson)

Figure 3.6. A linear planting along a watercourse. (Photo by Nicola Munro)

Figure 3.7. Plantings around paddock edges allow retention of open productive areas as well as habitat for wildlife. (Photo by David Lindenmayer)

limit the amount of sediment and fertiliser entering the water (Fig. 3.6). Linear plantings are better at performing these functions if they are relatively wide (at least 40 m).

Shape of a planting

Block-shaped plantings are the best for biodiversity because they are usually larger than strip-shaped plantings and their shape minimises the amount of edge. In addition, plantings that intersect with others tend to support more species of birds

Figure 3.8. Lerps on eucalypt leaves. In high numbers these can cause tree dieback. (Photo by David Lindenmayer)

Box 3.2. Edges, lerps and the Noisy Miner

An Australian native honeyeater, the Noisy Miner, has dramatically increased in abundance with the conversion of forest and woodland to farmland. It is an aggressive bird that chases away smaller species. When the Noisy Miner is removed from patches of remnant vegetation many species of small native birds quickly return. Many of these smaller birds eat lerps typically found on eucalypt leaves. Lerps are the sugary cover created by sap-sucking psyllid insects (Fig. 3.8). Large numbers of psyllids can cause tree dieback. Trees in areas with large numbers of Noisy Miners (and consequently few small lerp-feeding birds) often suffer dieback.

The Noisy Miner prefers edges of small patches of degraded woodland and forest. Large block-shaped plantings with minimal edges tend to support few Noisy Miners, especially if there is a dense understorey layer (e.g. of wattle trees).

than if they are isolated (see Chapter 2). This means where there are space constraints on a farm that might preclude the establishment of large block plantings, an alternative approach with positive outcomes for native wildlife is to establish intersecting strip plantings around paddock perimeters (Fig. 3.7).
In Box 3.2 we describe how block-shaped plantings, with a smaller amount of edge, can reduce presence of the aggressive native Australian honeyeater, the Noisy Miner (Fig. 3.9).

Figure 3.9. A Noisy Miner, a hyper-aggressive native honeyeater that is absent from large densely stocked plantings. (Photo by Julian Robinson)

Box 3.3. Breeding birds in plantings (by Suzi Bond, PhD student, ANU)

Recent work has indicated that some bird species prefer to nest 17 m or more away from the edges of a planting (Fig. 3.10). A 40 m wide planting would provide a 6 m wide band of interior area within a planting. Thus, plantings 40–60 m or more wide are likely to better support successful nesting. Plantings narrower than 40–60 m are not without value, even though there may be some species that will not nest successfully within them. Moreover, there may be subsequent opportunities to widen these planted areas with additional rows of adjacent trees and shrubs or to link narrow plantings with other plantings.

Which species to plant

If one of the objectives of a planting is to provide habitat for wildlife, re-creating similar plant species composition and structure to the original vegetation is valuable. This can be informed by examining nearby remnant vegetation characterised by similar topography and climate to the area targeted for planting. Natural bushland vegetation is inherently 'untidy'. There are plants of different ages and sizes, dead trees, logs, leaf litter and open areas with no trees or understorey.

Figure 3.10. A Crested Shrike-tit, a species that typically nests in the core (interior) of a planting. (Photo by Julian Robinson)

Figure 3.11. A Glossy Black-cockatoo, a species that feeds extensively in She-oak trees. (Photo by Julian Robinson)

To maximise the benefits for wildlife, we suggest a mix of plants that contains as many local native plants as is practical, including understorey plants, such as small shrubs, forbs, grasses and lilies, as well as native creepers and vines. We also suggest that the proportion of eucalypts in a planting should be similar to the proportion occurring in remnant native vegetation (often less than 20% of mid- and overstorey plants). Remnant vegetation is usually composed of many plant species, with the richest plant diversity usually found in the understorey.

In some cases there may be value in including particular species in a planting to attract particular kinds of animals or deter others. For example, plantings with Drooping She-oak may be more likely to become feeding sites for spectacular Glossy Black-cockatoos (Fig. 3.11). Similarly, specialist bark-foraging birds may be attracted to plantings where the eucalypt species have bark streamers. The presence of eucalypts in Buloke woodlands attracts Noisy Miners, so eucalypts should be reduced or avoided in Buloke plantings.

Ecosystem restoration plantings versus woodlot plantings

Recent research has compared the biodiversity gains of plantings that are similar to remnant vegetation (termed an 'ecosystem restoration planting') with simple plantings consisting only of trees (termed a 'woodlot planting'). Results showed that ecosystem restoration plantings support a greater range of bird and mammal species, including some rare species, than woodlot plantings. Furthermore, they are colonised by certain species sooner after establishment than woodlot plantings. For example, a restoration planting 4–8 years of age supports the same community

Figure 3.12. A Golden Whistler, a species that can occur in ecosystem restoration plantings comprised of many native plant species. (Photo by Julian Robinson)

of birds as a woodlot planting 11–15 years after establishment. In addition, woodlot plantings, even up to 26 years old, are dominated by generalist birds, such as the Magpie Lark, Red Wattlebird, Australian Magpie and Eastern Rosella. In contrast, ecosystem restoration plantings support more specialised species of birds associated with shrubby understoreys, such as the Superb Fairy-wren, Crested Shrike-tit, Brown Thornbill, Golden Whistler (Fig. 3.12) and Eastern Yellow Robin. Establishing ecosystem restoration plantings is particularly important in landscapes where the shrub cover has been degraded or removed (e.g. by grazing of remnants) or only woodlot plantings have been established.

As outlined above, there are clear biodiversity gains from establishing ecosystem restoration plantings. In addition, ecosystem restoration plantings have been shown to contain more carbon than woodlot plantings, they are better at preventing erosion, and are more effective at providing shelter from wind (see Box 3.1 on windbreaks). Ecosystem restoration plantings and woodlot plantings appear to be equally effective in mitigating problems associated with dryland salinity. However, ecosystem restoration plantings cost more to establish than woodlot plantings. This is because more plant species and a greater number of individual plants are generally established.

Density of plantings

The density of a planting can have a significant influence on its value for biodiversity. Research from the South West Slopes of New South Wales recently showed that dense plantings on hilltops do not support many reptile species, whereas sparse plantings do. Bats also avoid dense plantings. Other research has shown that dense plantings support shrub-loving bird species (Fig. 3.13).

Figure 3.13. A very dense planting, which may suit some species of animals, but not others. (Photo by Nicola Munro)

In pre-cleared landscapes, the density of trees would have been quite low on hilltops and plains (in many places estimated to be about 30 mature trees per hectare), with a higher density along watercourses. Shrub density may have been much higher on hilltops than on grassy plains. At a finer scale, native remnant vegetation tends to have some dense and some sparse patches, and also small clearings. Ideally, plantings should replicate this variability in density.

An ecosystem restoration planting that contains many understorey plant species will likely be planted more densely than a woodlot planting, although the tree component of both planting types may have a similar density. The density of plantings will also differ depending on how plants were established. Directly seeded plantings are frequently very dense, although they tend to naturally self-thin over time. We suggest that for tubestock plantings, trees and shrubs should be planted at a density similar to that found in nearby remnant native vegetation.

Including other features in a planting

It is possible to increase the biodiversity benefits of a planting by establishing it around important habitat features for wildlife, such as old trees, logs and rocks (Fig. 3.14). Plantings that contain existing old paddock trees have higher bird species richness than those without, and can fast-track animal colonisation. Big trees provide features that are otherwise absent from young plantings, such as hollows (for nesting

Figure 3.14. Plantings around existing old paddock trees can benefit the old tree, the younger planting vegetation, and wildlife. (Photo by Nicola Munro)

birds and possums), large streamers of bark that support a diverse assemblage of invertebrates eaten by mammals and birds, large horizontal branches (used as perching sites), large logs, and the local mycorrhizae (symbiotic fungi that help plants to grow well in poor soils). A paddock tree can also provide seed to promote natural regeneration of trees. The condition and life expectancy of a paddock tree may even be improved by surrounding it with a new planting; for example there may be more small birds to eat lerps and other insect pests (see Box 3.2).

Logs and rocks are also commonly used by wildlife, particularly reptiles and ground-foraging birds. Plantings with logs and rocks have higher bird and reptile species richness than plantings that lack these habitat attributes. However, pest animals such as the European Rabbit sometimes also use rocky areas, and control measures such as shooting and laying poison baits may be required.

References

Bird PR, Bicknell D, Bulman PA, Burke SJA, Leys JF, Parker JN, Van Der Sommen FJ and Voller P (1992) The role of shelter in Australia for protecting soils, plants and livestock. *Agroforestry Systems* **20**: 59–86.

Cleugh H (2003) *Trees for Shelter: A Guide to Using Windbreaks on Australian Farms.* Joint Venture Agroforestry Program. Rural Industries Research and Development Corporation, Canberra.

Cleugh H, Prinsley R, Bird PR, Brooks SJ, Carberry PS, Crawford MC, Jackson TT, Meinke H, Mylius SJ, Nuberg IK, Sudmeyer RA and Wright AJ (2002) The Australian National Windbreaks Program: overview and summary of results. *Australian Journal of Experimental Agriculture* **42**: 649–664.

Fischer J and Lindenmayer DB (2002) Small patches can be valuable for biodiversity conservation: two case studies on birds in southeastern Australia. *Biological Conservation* **106**: 129–136.

Kanowski J and Catterall CP (2010) Carbon stocks in above-ground biomass of monoculture plantations, mixed species plantations and environmental restoration plantings in north-east Australia. *Ecological Management and Restoration* **11**: 119–126.

Lindenmayer DB, Crane M, Michael D and Montague-Drake R (2007) Farmland bird responses to intersecting replanted areas. *Landscape Ecology* **22**: 1555–1562.

Munro NT, Fischer J, Barrett G, Wood J, Leavesley A and Lindenmayer DB (2011) Bird's response to revegetation of different structure and floristics – are 'restoration plantings' restoring bird communities? *Restoration Ecology* **19**, 223–235.

4

How to revegetate

Summary box

- There are two basic ways to establish a planting – from tubestock or by direct seeding.
- Good site preparation, especially weed control and fencing, is important for the success of both strategies.

Once the location, dimensions and composition of a planting have been decided, the next step is to determine which planting technique to use, and the site preparation required. This chapter focuses on different methods of establishing a planting, where to source plants, site preparation, weed control and fencing.

Different ways to establish a planting

There are two basic ways to get plants into the ground: by planting tubestock or by direct seeding. The most appropriate method will depend on soil type, rainfall and topography. It is important to consult a local Landcare group, Greening Australia representative, or Natural Resource Management body to find out what will work best in a given area. Discussions with farmers or restorationists with experience in revegetation also can be useful.

Planting tubestock

Tubestock plants are seedlings grown in a nursery from seed or cuttings (Fig. 4.1). They usually have a high survival rate (>80%) compared with direct seeding, so less seed is needed. However, tubestock are costly to produce and labour-intensive to grow and plant. Seed or cuttings must be collected, the plants propagated in nursery facilities, then each manually planted, usually with a tree guard and weed mat. Plantings established with tubestock are often characterised by unnaturally uniform rows.

In certain situations, planting tubestock is the best or only option for revegetation, such as in steep, rocky, or environmentally sensitive areas. Enhancement plantings (see Box 4.1) around existing remnant trees are also best done manually with tubestock to minimise disturbance to the remnant (Fig. 4.2). Some plants need to be propagated in nurseries; for instance, direct seeding is not appropriate for species that have fleshy fruit, or that reproduce by suckering.

Tubestock are usually planted individually into a hole and the soil tamped firmly around the plant (air pockets around the roots can dry them out and kill the plant). Holes can be created by ripping rows with a tractor (good for hard or

Figure 4.1. A tubestock seedling. (Photo by Nicola Munro)

Box 4.1. Enhancement plantings

In enhancement plantings, plants are added to an older planting or a patch of remnant vegetation, which can be beneficial where:

- remnants are degraded,
- shrubs and understorey plants have died, or
- an understorey was not originally established in a planting.

Enhancement plantings are usually conducted where natural regeneration is limited or absent.

Enhancement plantings often involve establishing or re-establishing an understorey. If an understorey has been damaged or lost, it is important to remove the cause, such as grazing stock or weed infestation. Be very careful with site preparation (e.g. weeding) to avoid disturbing the existing vegetation.

compact soils), or with a mattock or spade at sites that are unsuitable for tractors. Alternatively, holes can be made with specially designed tools, such as a Hamilton's tree planter – useful where soils are soft and haphazard placement of plants is desired (Fig. 4.3) – or the Pottipukti, a tube-shaped tool that creates a hole into which a plant is dropped and pressed into place without the operator having to

Figure 4.2. An enhancement planting on the South West Slopes of New South Wales. (Photo by David Lindenmayer)

Figure 4.3. A Hamilton's tree planter is a very useful tool for planting tubestock in soft soils. (Photo by Greening Australia Capital Region

bend over. It is important that holes do not have smooth sides as this prevents the roots from penetrating the surrounding soil. Greening Australia's Florabank website (http://www.florabank.org.au/) provides information on the different kinds of tools used to establish tubestock plantings.

It is important to keep the roots pointing downwards when planting tubestock, because roots that point up (j-rooting) will not grow strongly. Healthy tubestock from a nursery should not be root-bound (small plants are often better than large ones), and should have been 'hardened' (i.e. acclimatised to full sun and frost).

A tree guard placed over a plant will protect it from wind, grazing or browsing, frost, and dehydration. Tree guards also show where plants are located, which is important for subsequent weed control and to prevent trampling by people.

Surrounding a new plant with a weed mat or mulch will reduce competition with weeds. This can be very effective for up to two years, until they break down. Mats and mulch should be shaped to channel water to the stem.

Tubestock should be planted at a time of year that increases their chance of survival, for instance when it is wet and warm (i.e. no frost). Plants often require watering for at least the first few weeks after planting.

Direct seeding

Direct seeding is when seed is spread directly onto the ground. It can be done by hand, with purpose-built machines, by laying down branches with seed still attached, or using a method called 'hydromulching', in which a mixture of mulch, water and seed is sprayed onto the soil. Direct seeding is a cheaper way to establish a planting than with tubestock because there are no plant propagation costs. Plantings that have been direct seeded often look more natural as they are not characterised by uniform rows and a greater diversity of species can be established (Fig. 4.4). Direct seeded plants tend to have better root structure, which may improve the health and longevity of the plants. However, direct seeding sometimes results in low germination rates or slow establishment.

Direct seeding is the best option for very large sites. Mechanical seeders have been developed that scalp and rip the soil, sow the seed, and then cover the seed with soil (Fig. 4.5). Sophisticated mechanical seeders can spread different types of seed at different depths and add inoculants or smoke water (which promotes germination in some species). Organisations such as Landcare and Greening Australia have these kinds of machines for hire.

Direct seeding requires a large volume of seed, which can be costly to collect. Sourcing sufficient seed of local origin can be problematic, especially where there are limited bushland remnants to meet the requirements of large-scale revegetation projects.

Figure 4.4. A direct seeded revegetation site. (Photo by Nicola Munro)

Figure 4.5. A mechanical seeder. (Photo by Greening Australia Capital Region)

Figure 4.6. Preparing seed for planting. (Photo by Greening Australia Capital Region)

Box 4.2. Seed collection

In many cases, a landholder will acquire plants or seed from a commercial company or organisation such as Landcare or Greening Australia. However, it is possible for individuals to collect seed, and this may be a good option if there are sources of seed on a property. Three key aspects of seed collection from remnant vegetation should be observed.

The first is not to take too much seed. A general rule of thumb is to take only 10% of seed from 10% of plants of each species in a given patch of remnant vegetation.

The second is to maximise the genetic diversity of the seed by collecting from 20 to 100 plants of the same species in a patch, preferably from plants spatially separated by at least three times their height. This increases the chance that plants will be adapted to the range of conditions at a revegetation site.

Third, it is best to collect seed from sites that have similar soil, topography, climate, and altitude to the revegetation site. It is more important to match the conditions than to collect seed from the nearest site.

Once the plant material has been collected, seed can be extracted by putting nuts or pods in a bag (e.g. a pillow slip) in a warm, dry place until the nuts or pods open. Seed can then be 'cleaned', separated from the pods or nuts using a sieve (Fig. 4.6), and stored in a cool, dry place. Different plant species require different seed handling requirements, and remain viable in storage for varying lengths of time. Online resources, such as Greening Australia's Florabank website, provide background information on seed handling and storage. Clearly label seed with the date and the exact location and number of plants the seed was collected from to match seed source sites with revegetation sites and to track seed viability.

Permits are usually required to collect seed from public land and these can be obtained from the relevant government department.

Sourcing plants

The choice of plants is dependent on the goals of a planting. A good planting for biodiversity (an 'ecosystem restoration planting') requires many plant species of local origin, including shrubs, understorey and ground cover plants. The list of plants to be established in an ecosystem restoration planting should be based on the plant species that occurred at a site before it was cleared. If a planting is primarily for other purposes, such as a source of timber or firewood, shelter for stock, or to control salinity, then fewer species are required and they may not need to be local species (see Chapter 3 for a discussion of the different values of ecosystem restoration plantings and woodlot plantings).

Many plantings are established with financial and practical help from organisations such as Landcare, Greening Australia or a local Catchment Management Authority. These organisations are also a useful source of plants.

Figure 4.7. A nursery in which Australian native plants are propagated. (Photo by David Lindenmayer)

Material for direct seeding usually comes from seed banks, whereas tubestock are usually sourced from nurseries (Fig. 4.7). In both cases, an order of seed or seedlings may need to be arranged many months, if not a year in advance. This allows for seed to be collected at an appropriate time of year and, in the case of tubestock plantings, seedlings to be grown.

Seed banks are usually established by community organisations like Landcare or Greening Australia. They are a repository for locally collected seed. Seed banks

Box 4.3. Natural regeneration

In some situations, revegetation can be achieved by natural regeneration, in which seedlings emerge from seed stored in the soil or germinate from nearby remnant vegetation. Natural regeneration is by far the cheapest option for revegetation and resulting seedlings are genetically appropriate for the local conditions. However, regeneration that occurs naturally is usually composed of eucalypt trees without understorey species, and only takes place under specific conditions.

Natural regeneration will rarely occur under continuous grazing by stock, where there is heavy use of fertiliser, or where there is a dense cover of exotic grasses. Natural tree regeneration can be encouraged by removing grazing, or by rotational grazing with long rest periods, and low or no fertiliser use. Scalping or disturbing the soil also can also promote natural regeneration.

usually consist of a drying room or polyhouse (for drying seed or seed pods), and a cool store for the extracted seed. For a direct seeding project, a skilled seed bank manager will compile a seed mix based on the specific requirements of the planting.

Nurseries can be private businesses or can be run by community groups or non-government organisations. It is important to source plants from nurseries that specialise in native plants because they have expertise in propagating local vegetation. There are alternatives to sourcing plants from nurseries, such as the Trees For Life scheme in South Australia, in which volunteers grow plants that are then established on farmland. It is also possible to collect seed from a private property and propagate plants for personal use (see Box 4.2 on seed collection).

Site preparation

Different methods of establishing plants require different methods of site preparation. Site preparation involves reducing competition with non-native plants, controlling weeds, and sometimes reducing populations of animals, such as ants, which gather seeds, and wallabies, which browse on young plants.

For direct seeding, the planting area can be scalped to remove weed seeds (see below). The site can then be ripped (to break up the soil) and sown (Fig. 4.8).

Figure 4.8. Site preparation prior to establishing a planting. (Photo by David Lindenmayer)

For planting tubestock, competition with weeds can be reduced by scalping, spot spraying (Fig. 4.9) or using weed mats. Spot spraying needs to be done weeks or months in advance of planting, to ensure there is no residual herbicide. Weed mats can be used in conjunction with spot spraying (see below).

Weed control

Weed control is crucial before planting and the best results are achieved if it is done repeatedly for up to two years prior to establishing a planting. Reducing competition with weeds allows new seedlings to establish and helps limit long-term weed problems in a planting. The long-term management of plantings is discussed further in Chapter 5.

Weed control can include manual methods, such as scalping, chemical methods (herbicide), or barrier methods, such as weed mats or mulch. Scalping is the removal of the top layer of soil, which contains weed seeds, and can be very effective for direct seeding sites. Weed control is particularly important before direct seeding because once the seed is distributed, the precise location of individual plants is not known and weed control becomes difficult.

Figure 4.9. A steep and eroded site that has been spot sprayed in preparation for planting as shown by the patches of dead grass. (Photo by Nicola Munro)

Chemical methods of weed control include knockdown and residual herbicides. Knockdown herbicides (e.g. glyphosate) should be applied well before planting (usually the season before planting) when the weeds are actively growing. Residual herbicides (e.g. simazine, atrazine) should be applied two to four weeks before planting to kill weeds that have emerged following the application of a knockdown herbicide. It is important that the seedling roots do not contact soil with residual herbicide before it has broken down. This can be avoided by scalping the soil or creating a hole for the plant (e.g. with a planting tool). Roundup Biactive® is considered to be the only herbicide that is safe near waterways.

Weed mats are a good option in areas that are sensitive to the use of chemicals, although they are often also used after spot spray preparations. Weed mats are usually made of paper, jute or other biodegradable materials. They act as a physical barrier to weeds, and eventually break down to form mulch, which helps conserve moisture in the soil. However, weed mats can be expensive when used in large-scale revegetation projects.

Fencing

It is important to exclude domestic livestock from a revegetated area to eliminate browsing and trampling of new seedlings (Fig. 4.10). Intensive livestock grazing

Figure 4.10. Fencing around a planting protects it from stock. This fence has a gate and a stile for easy access. (Photo by Nicola Munro)

can also hinder natural regeneration and damage mature vegetation. Stock must be excluded for at least several years after establishment. Ecosystem restoration plantings may not tolerate stock at any time. Fencing is a large component of the total expenditure on a revegetation project, but costs can be reduced by strategic location of fences. For example, cutting off a corner of a paddock or locating a planting near an existing fence can reduce fencing costs.

Other browsing animals can also create problems in a planting. Rabbits and hares are notorious for nibbling the tops off seedlings. Rabbit and hare browsing can be reduced by using tree guards, or by population control (shooting, trapping, poisoning, or ripping burrows). Wallabies and kangaroos can also damage young plants and may need to be kept out or controlled. Note that permits are required to control native wildlife pests.

References

Dorrough J and Moxham C (2005) Eucalypt establishment in agricultural landscapes and implications for landscape-scale restoration. *Biological Conservation* **123**: 55–66.

Fischer J, Stott J, Zerger A, Warren G, Sherren K and Forrester RI (2009) Reversing a tree regeneration crisis in an endangered ecoregion. *Proceedings of the National Academy of Sciences* **106**: 10386–10391.

Greening Australia (2008) *Florabank*. Australia, <http://www.florabank.org.au/>.

Ralph M (1999) *Seed Collection of Australian Native Plants: For Revegetation, Tree Planting and Direct Seeding.* Bushland Horticulture, Melbourne.

Ralph M (2003) *Growing Australian Native Plants from Seed: For Revegetation, Tree Planting and Direct Seeding.* Bushland Horticulture, Melbourne.

5

How to maintain and manage a planting

Summary box

- It is important to regularly check a planting for weeds, and then control them.
- Dead trees and fallen logs make excellent habitat features and should be left in a planting wherever possible.
- Intensive livestock grazing is generally detrimental to the understorey of a planting and to biodiversity. Fences should be checked regularly and repaired where necessary to control grazing pressure.

Plantings require ongoing management after they have been established. In this chapter we discuss the need for ongoing weed control, why it is important to retain dead and fallen trees, and why livestock grazing should be controlled in plantings.

Weeding

The extent of weed problems in a planting depends largely on how well they were suppressed prior to establishment, and also how well weeds are controlled on the rest of the farm and on neighbouring properties. Weed control is not always easy in a planting, especially where there is a high density of plants, such as in ecosystem restoration plantings or where direct seeding was used for establishment. Herbicides need to be applied carefully, as native plants can be susceptible to their effects. Most native grasses, for example, die if glyphosate (a relatively mild

Figure 5.1. A Common Starling and Indian Mynas, exotic (pest) birds common in plantings with high levels of weed cover. (Photos by Julian Robinson)

herbicide) is used near them. If a planting is relatively small, it may be better to manually remove weeds for a few years.

It is important to regularly check plantings for weeds and remove them as soon as possible, as weeds can become a major problem very quickly. Many studies have shown that weed problems are best addressed in the early stages of infestation.

Recent research in southern Victoria has shown that weed cover decreases over time in ecosystem restoration plantings, but increases in woodlot plantings. This is another benefit of establishing ecosystem restoration plantings rather than woodlot plantings (see Chapter 3). In addition, plantings dominated by weeds attract introduced birds, such as the European Goldfinch, Common Starling and Indian Myna (Fig. 5.1), whereas revegetated areas dominated by native plants attract native birds. Thus, weed control is important not only for farm productivity and being a good neighbour, but also because it enhances biodiversity conservation.

Dead trees and fallen logs in plantings

Not all the plants in a planting survive in the long term. Shrubs and trees die for a range of reasons that includes pathogen or insect attack, insufficient mycorrhizal fungi on their roots, poor root structure, overcrowding, or a lack of water. In general, the loss of a few plants is not a problem, and natural self-thinning of vegetation can result in optimal density.

Although dead standing or fallen trees and shrubs can look 'untidy', they provide valuable habitat for animals and should be left wherever possible (Fig. 5.4).

Box 5.1. What is a 'weed'?

A weed is usually defined as a plant out of place. However, this definition is context specific and human centric. A weed to one person may not be to another. For example, sown pasture grasses, such as *Phalaris*, are considered weeds if they occur in a patch of remnant native vegetation. Native plants also can be weeds where they have spread beyond their original distribution (e.g. Cootamundra Wattle and Sweet Pittosporum). However, in most cases weeds are plants that have been introduced to Australia.

There are several classifications of weeds, including 'weeds of national significance', 'noxious weeds', 'environmental weeds' and 'agricultural weeds'.

Weeds of national significance are considered by Weeds Australia to be the worst weeds in the country, and are thought to require a national control approach. There are 20 listed plants that include Blackberry, Boneseed or Bitou Bush, Bridal Creeper, Gorse, Lantana, Serrated Tussock and Willow (Fig. 5.2).

Noxious weeds are considered to impact on agriculture, human health or the environment, can spread readily, but can be controlled reasonably effectively. They are usually required by law to be controlled by landholders. There are lists of noxious weeds for each state and Catchment Management Authorities often have their own lists.

Environmental weeds particularly effect native vegetation. These may be sown pasture plants or horticultural crops (e.g. olives), but can also be native plants that have spread beyond their original distribution. Environmental weeds out-compete local native plants and reduce habitat suitability for native animals. For example, willows along streams crowd out native vegetation, change water flows, increase erosion, and destroy habitat for native species, such as the Platypus (Fig. 5.3).

Agricultural weeds particularly effect agricultural production by reducing productivity of crops or pasture, or being toxic to livestock. Agricultural weeds cost landholders approximately $4 billion annually in lost production and weed control efforts.

Some weeds may be classified in more than one category. Blackberry, for example, is in all four categories. Agreement over the classification of weed species allows control to be more comprehensive, for instance, between adjacent properties.

Many plants that are now weeds in Australia were deliberately introduced by the horticultural and agricultural industries. Approximately 70% of weeds are escapees from domestic gardens, and many weed species now have restrictions on their sale.

Some birds prefer to nest in dead shrubs, and fallen branches and logs provide excellent sites for perching or foraging for many birds and reptiles. Dead and fallen trees and branches also provide habitat for often forgotten biodiversity, such as fungi and insects. The nutrients in fallen timber are eventually returned to the soil as an important part of nutrient cycling.

Figure 5.2. Serious weeds introduced into Australia: a) Blackberry, b) Boneseed or Bitou Bush, c) Lantana, and d) Willow. (Photos by Nicola Munro)

Grazing a planting

Stock grazing in plantings, especially high intensity set stock grazing, can cause substantial vegetation degradation. Structurally complex plantings or wetter sites may be particularly intolerant to grazing pressure and degrade within a short period of time. However, low intensity or rotational livestock grazing may be compatible with some simple forms of plantings such as woodlots, timber plantations, or plantings established under the WOPR scheme (see Box 2.6; Fig. 5.5).

Figure 5.3. A Platypus, a species negatively affected by weed species such as Willow that degrade stream banks. (Photo by Dave Watts)

Figure 5.4. Logs provide excellent habitat for many ground-dwelling animals and can be important structures around which to establish a planting. (Photo by Dave Blair)

Figure 5.5. Intensive stock grazing in a planting can have detrimental impacts on the ground and understorey layers. (Photo by David Lindenmayer)

Figure 5.6. Undertaking a field survey of birds in a planting. (Photo by Jenny Newport)

Damage by livestock can include removal of understorey vegetation, soil compaction, soil erosion, destabilisation of stream banks, and fouling of waterways. Overgrazing by domestic livestock can lead to vegetation becoming more open and can remove habitat for ground-dwelling animals or animals associated with understorey vegetation. Overgrazing may also promote weed infestation.

Appreciating a planting

Many interesting changes occur in a planting over time, particularly in the first 20 years (see Chapter 6). Many landholders enjoy following these changes. A good way to appreciate a planting is to spend time in it. Some landholders construct gates for easy access, and others even establish small paths, bridges and seats within a planting. Taking regular photographs or keeping a bird list adds to the appreciation of a planting and the changes that take place over time (Fig. 5.6).

6

How a planting changes over time

Summary box

- The structural complexity of vegetation increases rapidly for the first 20 to 30 years after establishment.
- Slow but important changes in a planting include the development of a leaf litter layer, the accumulation of large logs on the ground and the development of tree hollows.
- The diversity of plants in a planting is unlikely to increase of its own accord – enhancement plantings may be required to increase the habitat value for biodiversity.
- Many different animals can colonise a planting over time. The species richness and composition of animals in a planting will depend on its size and shape, total area, surrounding native vegetation, distance from other vegetation, structural complexity and floristic diversity, and the presence of features such as tree hollows and logs.

In this chapter we explore the changes that can be expected in a planting over time, such as the development of structural complexity in the vegetation, the development of a leaf litter layer, and colonisation by animals, such as native birds.

Development of structural complexity

The structural complexity of plantings increases rapidly for the first 20–30 years after establishment, after which it develops more slowly. Plant species grow at

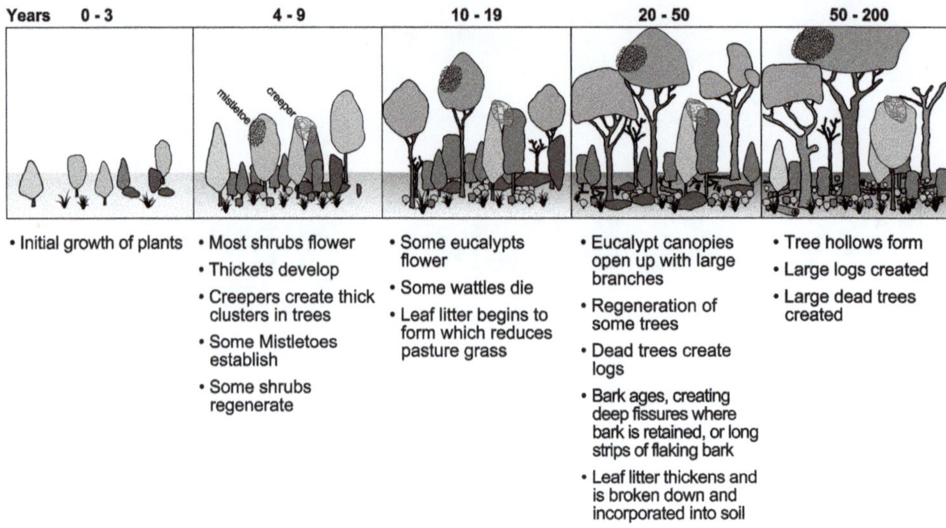

Figure 6.1. Changes in the structural complexity of planted vegetation over time. (Figure by Clive Hilliker)

different rates, which continuously alters the vegetation structure until all plants are mature. The plants may produce successful germinants, creating different age classes. As plants drop leaves and twigs, a leaf litter layer is formed. Some plants self-prune by dropping branches and others die and collapse creating logs and gaps in the canopy. These processes of development, self-thinning, mortality and reproduction lead to structurally complex vegetation comprising ground cover, understorey, shrub and tree layer plants of different condition, size and age (Fig. 6.1). A structurally complex planting usually attracts and supports more species of animals than a structurally simple planting (Fig. 6.2).

Colonisation of plantings by plants

Restoration practitioners may expect that when overstorey plants are established in a planting, the understorey will naturally be formed with no further management intervention, perhaps by wind or animal dispersed seed. However, research has shown that even after many years, there is almost no recruitment of non-planted native plants into revegetated areas. Therefore, if the objective is to create a planting with a wide variety of plant species, these species need to be planted deliberately at the outset (i.e. an ecosystem restoration planting) or subsequently established (i.e. an enhancement planting, see Box 4.1).

Most plantings are established with overstorey trees and understorey plants in the same seed or seedling mix. Some restorationists advocate putting the overstorey in first, and then planting the understorey several years later when conditions for understorey plants may have improved (for example, when there is more shade, less competition with pasture grasses, and more nutrients in the soil

Figure 6.2. A structurally complex planting. (Photo by Nicola Munro)

due to the presence of a leaf litter layer). However, there has been no research to date to determine which is the better approach to establishing an understorey.

Development of leaf litter, logs, hollows and mistletoe

The features that take the longest to develop in a planting are large logs, leaf litter, tree hollows and mistletoe. A layer of leaf litter can develop within a decade of a planting being established. Many Australian terrestrial ecosystems have a large amount of leaf litter, which can reduce competition with pasture grasses and weeds as well as provide habitat for many birds, mammals and reptiles.

Logs can only be as big as the trees they came from. Big old logs – critical habitat features for many birds, mammals, reptiles and invertebrates – derive from big old trees. It can take 50 to 100 years for a tree to be large enough to produce big logs through branch shedding or the collapse of a main trunk. The presence of large logs in a planting can be fast-tracked by establishing a planting around an old paddock tree or areas with scattered big logs, or by bringing them from elsewhere (Fig. 6.3). For example, old fence posts, fallen trees, or trees that need to be removed elsewhere on the property can be usefully translocated to a planting.

Figure 6.3. Paddocks with scattered logs can be good areas around which to establish a planting. (Photo by Jenny Newport)

Tree hollows are a critical resource for many Australian animals, but they are probably the slowest feature to develop in a planting. It can take 120 to 180 years for hollows to develop in eucalypts that are suitable for use by cavity-dependent animals, such as possums, gliders, cockatoos and large owls. A number of studies have demonstrated the biodiversity benefits of establishing revegetated areas around existing paddock trees. For example, bird species richness is significantly higher in plantings with paddock trees than in plantings without such large and important trees.

Erecting nest boxes is another way to provide cavities for hollow-dependent animals (Fig. 6.4). Nest boxes of different sizes and shapes placed at different heights can provide valuable nesting sites for a range of birds, possums and bats. However, artificial cavities have a limited lifespan and may need to be replaced at regular intervals (e.g. every 5–20 years). In addition, certain kinds of nest boxes can be occupied by introduced birds, such as the Common Starling and Indian Myna, or by European Honeybees. Special design features are needed to exclude these nest box pests; for example attaching carpet to the roof of a nest box prevents bees from establishing a hive. Several books and guides on how to build nest boxes for a range of Australian animals are listed at the end of this chapter.

Although very few plant species will naturally establish themselves in plantings, there are some that might. For example, after about 10–40 years, mistletoe may become established in a planting. Mistletoe is parasitic on tree hosts and is spread by birds, in particular, the Mistletoebird (Figs. 6.5 and 6.6). Mistletoe

Figure 6.4. A natural tree hollow and a nest box. (Photos by Nicola Munro)

Figure 6.5. Mistletoe, a key feature of native vegetation which can develop in a planting after 10–40 years. (Photo by Nicola Munro)

Figure 6.6. A Mistletoebird. (Photo by Julian Robinson)

can be a valuable part of forest and woodland ecosystems, as a source of nectar and fruit for birds, and dense foliage for nesting and cover from predators. Possums, gliders and insects eat the foliage of mistletoe.

While extensive mistletoe infestations can weaken or kill trees, they usually do so only in landscapes that are degraded or under severe ecological stress. In these cases, mistletoe can be cut from branches of a host tree, but this is rarely necessary.

Colonisation of plantings by animals

All plantings, no matter how small, provide habitat for some species of native animals. Even very young plantings (a year or so old) can support several species of birds (Fig. 6.7). Generalist bird species that prefer dense vegetation, such as the Superb Fairy-wren, are among the first to colonise new plantings (Fig. 6.8).

The extent of animal colonisation of a planting will depend on a number of factors. If a planting is structurally complex and has many plant species (e.g. an ecosystem restoration planting) then a range of bird species are likely to colonise it within five to ten years, including bird species of conservation concern, such as the Rufous Whistler and Red-capped Robin (Figs. 6.9 and 6.10).

Plantings established around old paddock trees are colonised by a greater diversity of birds and mammals than those without paddock trees. Plantings that

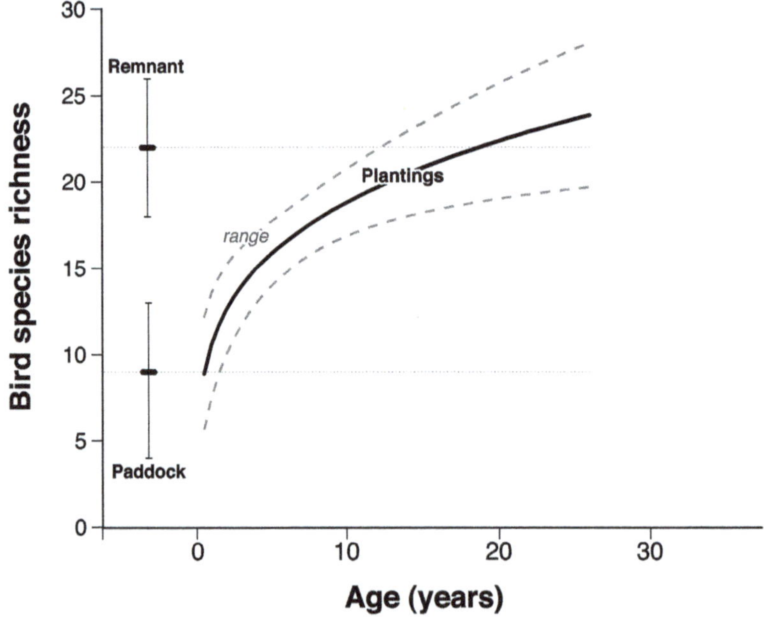

Figure 6.7. Plot from a study of birds in revegetation in Gippsland, showing how bird species richness increases over time. In this case, it took about 20 years for the average bird species richness in the revegetation to reach similar levels to remnant vegetation. The vertical lines show the range of, and average, bird species richness found in paddocks and remnants. (Figure by Clive Hilliker, adapted from Munro *et al.* 2011)

Figure 6.8. A Superb Fairy-wren, a bird often found in ungrazed young plantings. (Photo by Julian Robinson)

Figure 6.9. Red-capped Robins, spectacular birds of conservation concern that often occur in plantings. (Photo by Julian Robinson)

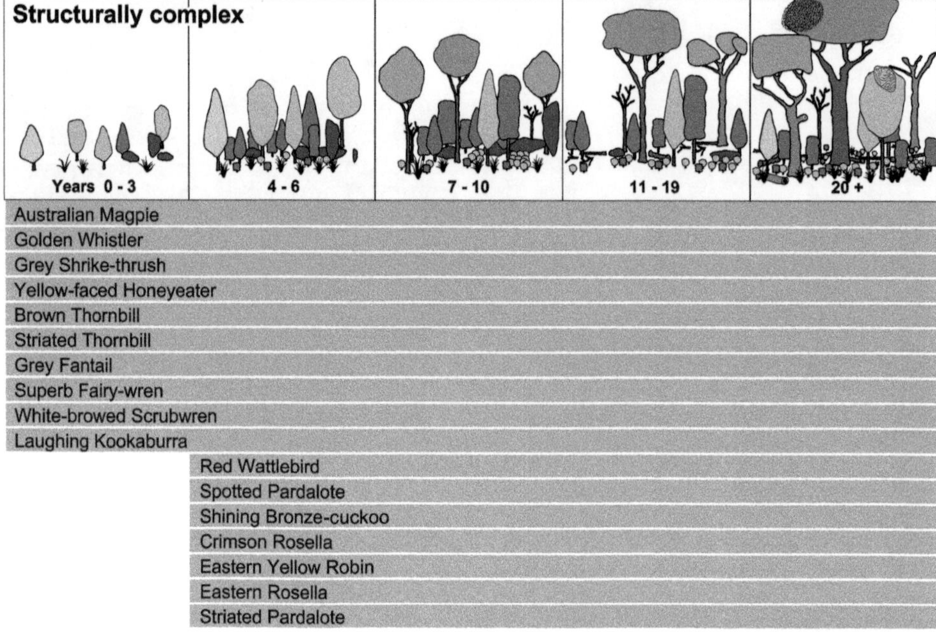

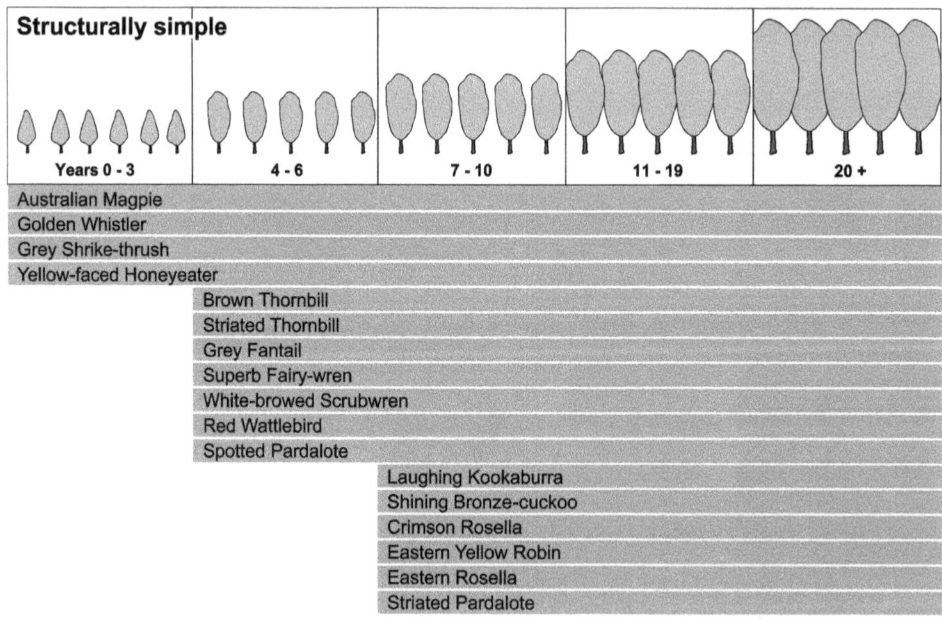

Figure 6.10. Bird species that colonised plantings in western Gippsland in the first ten years. Several species colonised structurally complex ecosystem restoration plantings sooner than structurally simple woodlot plantings. (Figure by Clive Hilliker)

Figure 6.11. The Koala (left) is known to move large distances across open paddocks, and the Squirrel Glider (above) is a species that is restricted in its movements in treeless areas. (Photos by Nicola Munro and Katherine Tuft)

Figure 6.12. An Eastern Whipbird, one of the species that has colonised the plantings in the Archies Creek region where an extensive revegetation program is underway (see Box 6.1). (Photo by Julian Robinson)

Box 6.1. Archies Creek restoration, Gippsland

The small farming region of Archies Creek in western Gippsland was long ago cleared of its majestic forests, leaving only a few mature trees. Forest clearing resulted in the loss of most forest animals. About 30 years ago, two families new to the area set about transforming the landscape. Today, there are extensive areas of revegetation running virtually the entire length of the Archies Creek watercourse with most local farmers contributing to this large-scale restoration effort.

The oldest plantings at Archies Creek (30 years old) are ecosystem restoration plantings that have been supplemented with enhancement plantings as new species became available from nurseries. By 2006, these plantings had begun to self-thin and were characterised by large logs and a thick layer of leaf litter interspersed with ground cover vegetation. Many of the plants had begun to self-propagate.

Despite there being around 7 km between the plantings and the nearest patch of remnant vegetation, the revegetated areas in the Archies Creek region now support populations of the Common Brushtail Possum, Common Ringtail Possum, Koala, Bush Rat, Agile Antechinus, Dusky Antechinus, Red-necked Wallaby, and Echidna as well as numerous birds, such as the Eastern Yellow Robin, Shining Bronze-cuckoo, Grey Fantail, Golden Whistler, White-browed Scrubwren, Leaden Flycatcher, Eastern Whipbird, Crested Shrike-tit and Brown Thornbill (Fig. 6.12). Most species of birds were found to be breeding in the revegetated areas.

More plantings are being established in the Archies Creek region every year, and the goal is to eventually link Archies Creek with the Powlett River, which is also being extensively revegetated (Fig. 6.13).

are wide or large are also likely to be colonised by more species than small or narrow plantings (see Chapter 3). In addition, plantings located close to other vegetation (remnants or other plantings) will be colonised by more species of birds than isolated plantings (see Chapter 2).

Bird colonisation of plantings has been studied quite widely; however, we know much less about rates of colonisation by other types of animals. Possums and gliders have specific requirements, such as tree hollows and particular kinds of food; reptiles require open spaces, rocks and logs; bats often prefer open canopies; and frogs need trees with water bodies nearby. The presence of these kinds of features within a planting is likely to accelerate their rate of colonisation by species in these groups.

Some species of birds are quick to colonise plantings because they are highly mobile. However, other species may be slow to colonise plantings; for example the Brown Treecreeper has specialised dispersal behaviour in which only one sex moves and the other remains where they were fledged and the species has rarely been found in plantings. Many mammals can cross surprisingly large areas of open farmland. The Koala has been known to cross up to 500 m of treeless paddocks

Figure 6.13. The Archies Creek revegetation project. (Photo by Nicola Munro)

(Fig. 6.11). Small vertebrates, such as reptiles, frogs, and small mammals may take a long time to colonise plantings even if habitat conditions are suitable because of difficulties in moving across areas of open farmland.

References

Casey K (1996) *Attracting Frogs to Your Garden*. Envirobook, Canterbury, NSW.

Franks A and Franks S (2004) *Nest Boxes for Wildlife*. Bloomings Books, Melbourne.

Grant J and The Gould Group (1997) *The Nestbox Book*. Wilkinson Publishing, Melbourne.

Munro NT, Fischer J, Barrett G, Wood J, Leavesley A and Lindenmayer DB (2011) Bird's response to revegetation of different structure and floristics – are 'restoration plantings' restoring bird communities? *Restoration Ecology* **19**: 223–235.

Munro NT, Fischer J, Wood J and Lindenmayer DB (2009) Revegetation in agricultural areas: the development of structural complexity and floristic diversity. *Ecological Applications* **19**: 1197–1210.

List of recommendations

Recommendation	Justification
Protect remnant vegetation	Remnant vegetation provides important habitat for native wildlife.
Fence remnants to control grazing pressure	Even small amounts of intensive grazing can damage remnant vegetation and make it less suitable for wildlife.
Create enhancement plantings if needed, but allow for natural regeneration first	Natural regeneration is cheaper and the seedlings are of local species and genetics.
Establish plantings that connect remnant vegetation or other plantings	Connectivity in the landscape can aid animal movement.
Establish plantings that are as large and as wide as possible	Large plantings usually have considerable variability in vegetation type and density and contain many wildlife species.
Plant a variety of trees, shrubs, understorey and ground cover and create dense and sparse patches	Greater structural complexity and patchiness provides more niches and thus habitat for more species of wildlife.
Try to match the pre-cleared vegetation structure, density and plant species composition	Matching local vegetation will provide more suitable habitat for local wildlife.
Plant as many local species as possible	Local plant species will be best adapted to local conditions.
Plant windbreaks	Windbreaks protect stock and crops.
Windbreaks should be semi-permeable with no gaps under the canopy	Wind tunnelling and eddies reduce the effectiveness of windbreaks.
Plant individual paddock trees	Paddock trees provide shelter for stock, wildlife habitat and connectivity, and reduce water tables.
Revegetate strategically to reduce water tables	Lowering water tables helps conserve remnant vegetation threatened by salinity, as well as protecting productive land.
Establish plantings along watercourses	Riparian plantings improve water quality, stabilise banks and provide wildlife habitat and connectivity.
Include features such as old trees, logs and rocks in a planting	These features provide good habitat for wildlife.
Resist the urge to 'tidy up'	Dead standing and fallen trees and shrubs provide structural complexity and important habitat features for wildlife.
Consider leaving rocky outcrops sparsely vegetated to provide reptile habitat	Planting rocky outcrops too thickly can reduce habitat for reptiles.

Further reading

For wildlife and revegetation see:

Bennett AF, Kimber S and Ryan P (2000) *Revegetation and Wildlife: A Guide to Enhancing Revegetated Habitats for Wildlife Conservation in Rural Environments.* Report no. 2/00. Bushcare, National Projects Research and Development Program, Canberra.

Hobbs RJ (1993) Can revegetation assist in the conservation of biodiversity in agricultural areas? *Pacific Conservation Biology* **1**: 29–38.

Kimber SL, Bennett AF and Ryan P (1999) *Revegetation and Wildlife: What Do We Know About Revegetation and Wildlife Conservation in Australia?* Environment Australia, Melbourne.

Lindenmayer DB, Knight EJ, Crane MJ, Montague-Drake R, Michael DR and Macgregor CI (2010) What makes an effective restoration planting for woodland birds? *Biological Conservation* **143**: 289–301.

Munro NT, Fischer J, Barrett G, Wood J, Leavesley A and Lindenmayer DB (2011) Bird's response to revegetation of different structure and floristics – are 'restoration plantings' restoring bird communities? *Restoration Ecology* **19**: 223–235.

Munro NT, Fischer J, Wood J and Lindenmayer DB (2009) The effect of structural complexity on large mammal occurrence in revegetation. *Ecological Management and Restoration* **10**: 150–153.

Munro NT, Lindenmayer DB and Fischer J (2007) Faunal response to revegetation in agricultural areas of Australia: a review. *Ecological Management and Restoration* **8**: 200–208.

Ryan P (1999) The use of revegetated areas by vertebrate fauna in Australia: a review. In *Temperate Eucalypt Woodlands in Australia: Biology, Conservation, Management and Restoration.* (Eds RJ Hobbs and CJ Yates.) pp. 318–335. Surrey Beatty & Sons, Chipping Norton, NSW.

For revegetation of other ecosystems in Australia see:

Grant P (2003) *Habitat Garden.* Australian Broadcasting Corporation, Sydney.

Peel B (2010) *Rainforest Restoration Manual for South-Eastern Australia.* CSIRO Publishing, Melbourne.

Romanowski N (2009) *Planting Wetlands and Dams.* 2nd edn. Landlinks Press, Melbourne.

Romanowski N (2010) *Wetland Habitats: A Practical Guide to Restoration and Management.* CSIRO Publishing, Melbourne.

Salt D, Lindenmayer DB and Hobbs R (2004) *Trees and Biodiversity: A Guide for Australian Farm Forestry.* Joint Venture Agroforestry Program, Rural Industries Research and Development Corporation, Canberra.

Staton J and O'Sullivan J (2006) *Stock and Waterways: A Manager's Guide.* Land and Water Australia, Canberra.

For restoration of remnant vegetation see:

Bradley J (2002) *Bringing Back the Bush: The Bradley Method of Bush Regeneration.* New Holland Publishers, Chatswood, NSW.

Buchanan R (2009) *Restoring Natural Areas in Australia.* Industry and Investment NSW, Orange, NSW.

For other guides to encouraging wildlife on farms see:

Lindenmayer DB, Archer S, Barton P, Bond S, Crane M, Gibbons P, Kay G, MacGregor C, Manning A, Michael D, Montague-Drake R, Munro N, Muntz R, Okada S and Stagoll K (2011) *What Makes a Good Farm for Wildlife?* CSIRO Publishing, Melbourne.

Lindenmayer DB, Claridge A, Hazel D, Michael D, Crane M, MacGregor C and Cunningham R (2003) *Wildlife on Farms.* CSIRO Publishing, Melbourne.

For the ecology of forests and woodlands see:

Kirkpatrick JB (1994) *A Continent Transformed: Human Impact on the Natural Vegetation of Australia.* Oxford University Press, Melbourne.

Lindenmayer DB and Beaton E (2000) *Life in the Tall Eucalypt Forests.* New Holland Publishers, Chatswood, NSW.

Lindenmayer DB, Bennett AF and Hobbs R (2010) *Temperate Woodland Conservation and Management.* CSIRO Publishing, Melbourne.

Lindenmayer DB, Crane MJ and Michael D (2005) *Woodlands: A Disappearing Landscape.* CSIRO Publishing, Melbourne.

For other practical revegetation guides see:

Department of Sustainability and Environment (2006) *Native Vegetation – Revegetation Planting Standards – Guidelines for Establishing Native Vegetation for Net Gain Accounting.* DSE, Melbourne.

Greening Australia (2003) *Revegetation Techniques: A Guide for Establishing Native Vegetation in Victoria.* Greening Australia, Victoria.

Stelling F (Ed.) (1998) *South West Slopes Revegetation Guide.* Murray Catchment Management Committee and Department of Land and Water Conservation, Albury.

Index

Figures in bold type refer to illustrations.

www.ingramcontent.com/pod-product-compliance
Lightning Source LLC
LaVergne TN
LVHW060632110826
845147LV00014B/897

9780643103122